# The

# Flourishing

# **HOME**

## Inspired Places, Enlightened Lives

# The
# Flourishing
# HOME

## Inspired Places, Enlightened Lives

### Julie DeEsch-Kaminski, MA

COGENT PUBLISHING NY

IMPRINT OF THE WHITSON GROUP, INC.

Published by Cogent Publishing NY
Imprint of The Whitson Group, Inc.
3 Miller Road, Putnam Valley, NY 10579
www.cogent-publishing.com

Manufactured in the United States of America
First Edition

Front cover painting: Jodi Ohl
Front cover design: DesignSpinner, www.designspinner.com

ISBN: 978-0-925776-35-8
1 2 3 4 5 6 7 — 18  17 16 15 14

*To my husband Jay, my children, Trevor, Tristan and Gabrielle,*
*and my parents, Chris and Jess*

# CONTENTS

# INTRODUCTION

When the contractor who built your home started work, he went through a number of steps. First the foundation had to be built. The framework went up before the drywall and siding were added. Along the way, workers used a blueprint to guide their efforts. At the end of the process, they had built a home that is safe, stable, and that will last for decades. But a house is just a building until people move in. Only when you started living there did your house become a home.

Now, there are a ton of books on the shelves about redecorating and landscaping. *The Flourishing Home* is a far different kind of guide. Together, you and I will use wickedly simple, easy and inexpensive tools and techniques to make your home work for you. Along the way you'll grow happier, healthier and sexier. And who doesn't want that!

Creating the Flourishing Home is about making life easier. It's about enhancing your wellness and your sense of wellbeing. Whether your home is a mirror that reflects your personality, a place for renewal, or a sanctuary, everything under your roof matters. You, your spouse, your children and your friends deserve to step into a house that is more than a structure. While a Flourishing Home can't make you exercise, eliminate that annoying neighbor or create the perfect job lead, the quality of your home environment impacts all these areas…whether you're aware of how it works or not.

As a middle-aged mother of three balancing family, marriage, work, home and self, the ideal lifestyle is somewhat… elusive. I struggle to maintain a healthy weight. I have a tendency to yell after the third time asking a child to do homework. In the evenings when I'm exhausted, I put bedtime before time with my husband. I am frustrated when I can't enjoy the things I love.

Truly there is no single magic answer. But there is a simple, easy method that can create a Flourishing Home. By tweaking the home environment, we can make it easier to maintain a healthy weight, holler less, and enjoy some downtime with loved ones. Although our list of needs, wants and goals will constantly change, the basic quest for wellness and wellbeing can become far less challenging.

Making your home work for you becomes much easier if you build a solid foundation, erect the framework, and draw up a blueprint. The foundation is critical to achieving the best possible home for you and your family. A house built on an unstable foundation will crumble over time.

*The Flourishing Home* will help you build a strong foundation by translating values and pleasurable feelings into characteristics that fill your home environment. After defining those critical components, we will create a unique blueprint/framework from which you can work. You are unique, your home is unique, and so your solutions will be tied to your personal values, desires, strengths, obstacles and, ultimately, your solutions.

I started doing this work after walking a life path that led me through several different fields. After an early business career, I realized I could be both a professional and a parent. I received my master's degree in counseling psychology and welcomed my first child into the world. Although I loved helping people, dealing with their sadness every day became overwhelming, so I returned to teaching group fitness and personal training.

Over the years, my various areas of expertise began to merge. I realized the importance of attending to all aspects of wellness and wellbeing. As I began offering workshops, I recognized that many of the topics centered on the home. Every space in your home, whether it's a formal dining room, a master bedroom oasis or the narrow entryway at your front door, can be inspired and inspiring. When you create a Flourishing Home, the whole of your life is enlightened.

This powerful dynamic works for individuals from every walk of life. Over the years, I've worked with single parents raising kids alone, people who lost their mates, seniors, traditional and blended families, and even children. Their needs have ranged from honoring a family member who has died to celebrating joyful milestones and beyond. Together we have created loving, nurturing, supportive, festive, restful, healing and healthy environments. We created Flourishing Homes!

If I could, I would walk into every house in America to help people transform their environments. Since I can't possibly do that in just one lifetime, I've written the book you're holding now. This book will help you explore your desires, spark your awareness of different needs, and set goals based on new knowledge. I'll ask questions, offer solutions, and help you brainstorm ideas that are all your own. At some points you'll find yourself taking tiny steps and at others you'll make big leaps. Either way, you'll constantly move toward a happier, healthier and sexier home.

Each chapter will tackle a different topic. We'll look at "primes," the things that trigger certain behaviors, and adjust them so they prompt you to take positive action. The "transition points" in your home will be of special interest because they influence how you feel when you leave the house and when you return home. The views your environment offers will be modified so they please all of your senses. Separate chapters will consider "hubs," "hearts," and "fueling stations." By the time you create your own blueprint, you'll have all the tools you need to optimize your wellness and wellbeing. Maybe, you'll even enjoy a few giggles along the way!

---

### Idea Spark: Blue Sky Thinking

If you could be granted three wishes that would change or improve your home, what would they be? Why?

---

CHAPTER ONE

# FOUNDATIONS

---

*The Flourishing Home* will create a happier, healthier, sexier you...
but what exactly is happy, healthy and sexy? To understand the heart of
these concepts, recognize that this book is not about building a house; it's
about building a home. A house is just a structure made of brick and mor-
tar and plaster. A home uses stones quarried from the bedrock of your
desires, your goals and your needs.

The Flourishing Home—the happy, healthy, sexy home—provides
stability, confidence and security. The Flourishing Home begins and ends
with you.

---

**Idea Spark: Have a conversation with your home**
- What does your home want to tell you?
- What does your house like?
- What does your house dislike?
- If your home had three wishes, what would they be?

---

## Health = Wellness

True health encompasses all aspects of wellness. For many people,
wellness is a holistic approach to good psychological health, excellent
physical health, and satisfaction or peace with their lives and themselves...
in other words, the balance of the mind, body and spirit. Some people
might consider that a fad. It might even seem like a touchy-feely rehash
of the hippy mantra about peace and love. Put aside that baggage for a
moment and really think about how wellness is becoming more valuable
in our modern society.

These days, more businesses and organizations are demonstrating how much they value wellness through programs that aim to prevent disease and manage healthcare costs. Although the cynic might say all their efforts are driven by the bottom line, financial health is part of the wellness picture. And if accountants make it possible for employees to exercise at an on-site gym, who cares why? What counts is that employees are being given easy access to personal wellness!

These definitions of wellness are only two of the many available. The essence of wellness can be captured by defining it as a construct. Constructs are complex ideas. Because they exist only as ideas, they are difficult to measure in the real world. Weather is a perfect example. The weather at any given point in time is made up of several elements. Cloud cover, temperature, the amount of moisture in the air, wind speed, even the amount of sunlight reaching the Earth combine to create weather.

A home can also be a construct. A house (which is just a building) can contain many elements necessary for living without ever becoming a home. A hotel offers a place to sleep, a bath and sink, lighting, chairs and even entertainment, but it's hardly a place to call home. A house in the suburbs is just another building surrounded by grass if it lacks the elements that will make it a home.

On the other hand, places that have few amenities can make fine homes. A city apartment can feel warm and welcoming. A coffee shop can become a home office as easily as a repurposed bedroom. And how often have you heard someone talk about a church, or a spot where friends gather, as a "home away from home?" Home, then, is a construct made up of many different elements.

Wellness is also made up of different types of elements, such as décor, peace, comfort, and satisfaction with the atmosphere. When combined, these elements become wellness. But if wellness is more than one thing, how can we measure or observe it? Mmm... that's clearly going to be tricky. On the other hand, if we can define the different elements that make up wellness, then we're getting somewhere.

## Wellness in the Flourishing Home

This part of the foundation is made up of five different stones. Although you might chose to focus on one at a time, no single stone is more important than the other. They fit together perfectly to form the heart of the Flourishing Home.

### 1. Stress Management

Life is stressful. Believe it or not, there is such a thing as good stress, also called eustress. Good stress comes from the excitement and pressure of stretching yourself to your maximum limits. We experience good stress when we juggle all the details required to buy a new house or start a new job. Whether it's good or bad, there will always be some elements of stress in your life.

And, of course, there are the truly negative kinds of stress. Any event that triggers the fight-or-flight response is negative stress. It can be as obvious as realizing someone is following you through the parking lot or as subtle as dealing with an irritating neighbor. Chronic stress, the kind that continues to be in your life for a long period of time, can trigger heart disease or high blood pressure. It also causes anxiety in the mind and unsettles the spirit.

Both good and bad stress must be managed. Straightforward efforts include getting a good night's sleep and decluttering your living space. Other efforts, like working through the argument you're having with that irritating neighbor, are more personal. In another chapter, we'll address common areas of stress in depth and take a look at specific, easy ways to manage the good and the bad.

### 2. Spiritual Refueling

To experience the full, positive effects of true wellness, it's important to fill your spiritual tank. For some, religion is the fuel. Your tank can also be filled outside the church, synagogue or temple. The beauty found during a walk in nature, while contemplating art at a museum or gallery, and the soft warmth of a purring cat are all sources. The places, things and activities that will refuel you are unlimited and intensely personal. The key is becoming mindful of opportunities you can incorporate into your life. In later chapters, I'll show you how some of the people I've worked with have set up their home refueling stations and provide some simple ideas for implementing your own.

### 3. Eating Behaviors and Nutrition

Although both these items deal with food, they show up in our lives in different ways. Eating behaviors include positive actions like eating when you are hungry and stopping when you are full. They also include negative things like eating when you are stressed, unhappy or bored. We've all reached for the chocolate on at least one stressful day!

Nutrition includes having a healthy diet. Personally, I think dieting is for the birds. The real goal is to find ways to eat the best foods and to maintain our optimal weight… for life. In this arena as in so many others, what works for one person will not work for another. The diet books offer different programs…eat carbs, don't eat carbs; sugar is the enemy; raw foods are the savior; the Atkins diet, the Zone, the grapefruit diet, the soup diet. You could read a book every week for a year and still not put a dent in this bookshelf!

Fortunately, the tools and tactics for improving eating behavior and nutrition aren't nearly as complicated as all those books make them appear. *The Flourishing Home* will provide you with all the tools and tips you need to create "personalized eating" and a nutrition plan that serves you and your family.

### 4. Fitness and Activity

The latest research shows that fitness isn't only about exercise. To make sure you're getting the maximum benefits, you have to consider your overall activity level. An athletic person who faithfully works out at the gym or runs six times a week might end up with a perfect body, but if they sits at a desk for hours at a time, she might be worse off than the person who never exercises yet is active all day.

When thinking about formal exercise, the current recommendation is one hour per day for middle-aged women who want to maintain their current weight. Yikes! I've got a lot of catching up to do, and I'm you do too. Remember, though, that we don't have to rely solely on pumping iron or running marathons to maximize our wellness. The level, type, and results will be different for each person. Later chapters offer tools and tactics to optimize your exercise routine and activity level in a balanced, healthy way…and you won't have to feel like you're training for the Olympics!

### 5. Health and Medical Concerns

In the Flourishing Home, conditions like high cholesterol, cancer, arthritis and other ailments combine with personal characteristics such as genetics, gender and age. These very real factors can influence our overall wellness. Compare the needs of an individual battling cancer to those of a young athlete. The strengths, hurdles and strategies for optimal health are different for each person. Peak performance for the athlete might be running a personal best while peak performance for a person in remission might be a walk around the block.

Nutritional needs can also vary widely. A person who has high cholesterol or diabetes will address nutrition differently than the person who has no diet-dependent issues. Someone with Crohn's disease can experience perfect health by avoiding a few key types of foods. An individual with a family history of osteoporosis will consume more dairy products.

An entire chapter of this book is dedicated to tools and tactics that will improve or manage common and unique health and medical aspects. Even if your specific issues aren't addressed, you'll find enough ideas to help you create a personalized system that will lead to total wellness.

## Happiness = Wellbeing

In the Flourishing Home, happiness encompasses all aspects of wellbeing. To be happy means that you have reached a level of comfort and success in all the aspects associated with wellbeing. That doesn't mean you won't keep improving in one area or that you will never experience problems in your Flourishing Home. It does mean you have achieved balance.

*Since wellbeing is also a construct—something that isn't easily defined because it's an idea—we'll have to consider each of its parts individually. Fortunately, psychologists who study these kinds of things have already done the hard work for us. They have found that wellbeing contains five elements.*

### 1. Positive Emotions

Well, here we are with another phrase that could mean just about anything! The definitions of positive emotions will be as varied as the people reading this book. By determining whether or not we are happy—truly happy, meaning comfortable, satisfied, content, encouraged, inspired and joyful—we find out that our home is flourishing... or floundering.

In later chapters, you'll find plenty of examples of how my clients have created true happiness in their home environments. The tools and techniques offered as we move forward will help you bring positive elements into your home to support your happiness...no matter how you define it!

## 2. Engagement

Yes, you guessed it...this definition is also subjective. The things that make you feel engaged are not going to match those of your spouse, your children, or your best friend. However, for this book we can define engagement as a flow state. When you achieve a flow state, you are immersed in an almost single-minded focus. You are entirely focused (i.e., engaged) in one activity or way of being. In the Flourishing Home, you are living a life that is passionate and exuberant, a life that unfolds like a garden in bloom.

## 3. Meaning

To fully understand this aspect of wellbeing, let's consider the difference between meaning and purpose.

Having a purpose in life means that you have a single goal for all your years on Earth. You might want to look back before you die and think, *Yes, my job at the elementary school touched the minds of many children,* or *All those years of volunteering at the food bank eased the burden of poverty among my fellow human beings.* Many people think that their purpose in life will lead them to a meaningful life, but a life's purpose isn't the only thing that creates meaning.

In the Flourishing Home, meaning is built right into the foundation. Every part of your house should contribute to what is most important in your life. The effort you spend on making your home a fortress against the stresses of the external world is meaningful to your family. Creating a private retreat in your bedroom is meaningful to you. The nutrition a parent provides while packing the kids' school lunches is meaningful to the children... despite how often they complain about carrots instead of cupcakes for dessert!

Your house might end up with a lot of tools that support your purpose in life or many reminders of why you're on this Earth. That's great, and that certainly creates meaning for you as you work toward that goal. In the Flourishing Home, every object and space can become meaningful in some way. When this happens, your house becomes both an oasis and a headquarters. It supports the best of who you are and who you are becoming. And that's clearly a part of wellbeing.

### 4. Accomplishment

This aspect of wellbeing has two important components. First, of course, is that the Flourishing Home will support your movement toward accomplishing your goals. I want you to expand your thinking. The goals you have for becoming a more attentive spouse, a better parent, a more compassionate neighbor or a loyal friend are all supported in the Flourishing Home.

Second, you absolutely must recognize and validate your past accomplishments. You didn't get where you are without a lot of hard work and dedication. By honoring your prior accomplishments, you recharge your dedication to reaching new goals. No matter where you are in life, you have already accomplished something. Everyone has something to be proud of!

### 5. Positive Relationships

Do you have a place to gather comfortably with friends and family, a place that will foster positive relationships, which in turn will influence positive emotions? Too often, people allow their home environment to become so negative or stressful that it works against their wellbeing. Negativity and stress don't have to be caused by big, dramatic things like arguments with family members or a health crisis. People are suffer because of the most subtle things imaginable.

In the chapters ahead, we'll see how the obligation to keep even a small gift from a friend or relative can be a burden. Beige paint on the walls of a woman who loves bright colors might be part of why she feels so blah when she arrives home. The mess of misplaced tools, half-finished home repair projects, and stacks of garbage that greet a man as he pulls into the garage can contribute to the heavy feeling he gets when he arrives at the place that should be his retreat.

An environment filled with negativity and stress not only impacts your happiness, it can keep you from being engaged, eliminate any meaning, impede your accomplishments and tangle your relationships. *The Flourishing Home* eliminates the negative things in your environment and replaces them with happy, healthy, sexy options that reflect the real you.

Which brings us to the final aspect of a truly Flourishing Home.

## Sexiness = Living Your Best Life

Now to define the one you've all been waiting for… sexy! Don't worry; this concept isn't something you'll find splashed across the cover of the latest women's magazine. It's not about weight, age or appearance. I won't tell you to hang red velvet drapes in your bedroom or set up a dance pole in your workout room.

This might be the most personal concept in this entire book. For our purposes, sexy means living the best life possible. It's about thriving. It's about building a confident, rock-the-world attitude. A sexy attitude brings a special spark to everything you do inside and outside your home. It supercharges your life and the way you live. When your foundation includes a sexy attitude, you can launch into your life with the fire of passion!

We won't actually explore sexy in depth in this book. Instead, you'll discover sexy on your own by improving your wellness and wellbeing. Living your best life is sexy!

## Simple and Individual

The three concepts we've worked with so far—happy, healthy and sexy—are the foundation of the Flourishing Home. Having only three primary areas means the process of creating a truly supportive home environment is simple. Considering how busy we all are these days, simple is great!

Since two of these concepts have five components each, you have eleven different areas to work with. You can opt to work with all eleven at once or select a few to start. You may have some areas already well taken care of and don't need to readdress them. But if you look at all the ways these eleven different areas can be combined, you come up with something just shy of 40 million choices. Wow! Bet you didn't expect that when you picked up this book!

No matter who you are or what you're hoping to find, these simple ideas can be tailored to your exact specifications. The Flourishing Home is an environment that supports, nurtures, and inspires you.

## Framework

Now that we have defined the core building blocks of your foundation, we need to make the framework personal. Your picture of wellness is unique to you. The pieces you'll select and the way you'll put them together will be like no one else's. It's as if you're getting ready to look through the jigsaw puzzle of choices for paint, carpet, curtains, furniture, cabinets, appliances and doorknobs. Most of us have a general idea of how we want things to look. One person will prefer earth tones and rustic décor while another will want industrial steel and glass. Each person will throw out catalogues that don't have anything like what they want before looking through the ones that offer the best choices.

Let's start by looking through your catalogs to discover, define and develop your likes and dislikes. We do this by considering how you feel in your current environment and how you want to feel once you have implemented some sort of change. We'll also consider personal and family values, real and perceived obstacles, and strengths. Finally we will put together a blueprint or action plan for improved wellness and wellbeing and a rock-the-world lifestyle. Ready? I am!

**Appreciative Inquiry**

The most important part of this process is to focus on positive things. Tune into what is working well.

- What do you love?
- Which is your favorite room? Why?
- Which room do you gravitate toward? Why?
- Do you have a favorite chair? Why?
- What are your five favorite objects in the house? In each room?
- Which other homes you visit appeal to you? Why?
- What works well in those homes?
- What are your desires?
- What motivates you?

## Strengthen the Foundation

What do you want your home to feel like? We're not talking about the way things look but about the atmosphere. For a moment, table any concerns you might have about square footage or budget. An unlimited decorating budget can make a home look pretty but it might not feel good to live there.

When you walk into your home, you immediately have some sort of reaction to the environment. Low lighting can make one person feel trapped while it makes another person feel cozy. An extensive collection of figurines inherited from a relative can be a source of pride or a cluttered burden. The source of the feelings isn't important right now. The only things you need to ask are how your current environment makes you feel and what you want your home to feel like.

It's also important to consider that the feeling in each room may be different depending on how the room is used. This becomes clear when you think about how people behave in certain environments. Visitors to a library behave differently than people on a playground. In other words, the way we behave is influenced by our environment. How do you want to behave in your home? Is your house a private space or does it also serve as a gathering place for neighborhood friends?

When asked to describe her house, Brenda said, "empty... too big... in need of decoration." When asked how she would like it to feel, she responded, "cozier, more intimate, more natural, uncluttered closets." We brainstormed a wish-list of items that would create those positive feelings. To make things cozy, she's keeping an eye out for soft throws and plush rugs. To pull in more natural aspects, she's hunting for low-maintenance plants and decorations like dried grasses, pussy willow branches and eucalyptus stems.

To start, work with these basic questions:
- What is your favorite room in the house? Why?
- What about that room makes you feel good?
- What colors represent that feeling?
- What textures create that feeling?
- What kind of lighting generates that feeling?
- What smells make you feel good?
- What sounds will create that feeling for you?

Use this list with everyone who lives in your house, even the youngest members of your family. You might be surprised by what your kids reveal! One time I worked with a twelve-year-old who had lost her mother to cancer. Our goal was to create a nurturing space so she could move forward by living in a soothing environment. Before entering the room, we chatted about her personality, her likes, and what made her happy.

She described herself as energetic and "spazy." She liked bright blues and greens, and wanted a room that would be "quirky." Then we went on to talk about what she liked and what she didn't like. Her room had an Asian flair. An Oriental light fixture dominated the middle of the room and Zen-inspired art hung on the walls. A color pallet of jade and black had been used throughout. The room was as far from her personality as Japan is from America!

**Feeling**

List the rooms you wish to work with, then ask:

- What do I want to feel in each room?
- Ask the same question of each person who lives in your home.
- What do I want my guests to feel in each room?

With a limited budget, we transformed her room into an environment in line with her desires and personality. The Asian artwork came down and the light fixture was pulled. A fresh coat of blue paint accented the walls and she created a quirky light fixture using beads she had on hand. The mini-makeover generated a totally new energy that supported her by reflecting what made her happy.

## Values

Every time I open a home magazine and see a beautiful two-page spread labeled "dream room," I can't help but frown. No matter how bright and airy the space, those models always look so sterile. They might be pretty but they don't tell you much about the people who live there. The Flourishing Home reflects your individual values and those of your entire family.

If you doubt this, peek at your friends and family members. Not their homes, but the people themselves. Although we might know all our neighbors on a first-name basis, we tend to befriend those who share our individual and family values. Our close friends certainly share a substantial portion of our value systems, and the coworkers we like best usually share at least a few of our values. The place where you spend a substantial portion of your day should reflect your most important values.

Putting those values into words may be difficult at first. Pay attention to activities you and your family tend to repeat. For my clan, spending time together is important. We love beach vacations and over the years, we have accumulated a number of family pictures framed in seashell borders. As our family matured, our trips became more adventurous. Our photo books are stacked on the coffee table and individual pictures cover the wall.

**Values**

- What are your family values?
- What are the values of each person living in the home?
- What are the hobbies, preferences, interests of the family as a whole? Of each family member?

We also value education; each child had a desk in his or her room, but since no one likes to work alone, the desks weren't being used. We turned the living room into a music/study hall/office for the children. Rather than an unused stagnant space, that room became a vibrant hub. The entire downstairs now has a welcoming energy that reflects how highly we value education. Don't be afraid to repurpose your spaces to reflect your values.

## Why the Flourishing Home is So Important

While your home can't exercise for you, it can support your efforts to live the best life possible. Positive psychology gives us the Happiness Formula: 50% of happiness is determined by our genetics, our early conditioning, and our heredity. Another 10% springs from living conditions. The remaining 40% depends on choices we make for personal fulfillment or to achieve our intentions. While we can't do much about the first half, fully 50% can be manipulated in the home.

When your outer reality matches you inner desires, your inner desires have a greater chance at fulfillment. After dealing for eight hours with meetings, emails, phone calls, a minor confrontation with a peer, and a forty-five minute commute, you want (and frankly need) a peaceful respite. You're looking forward to a place that lets your tense shoulders relax...only to be met by a pile of dirty laundry when you open the door. If the first sight in your environment is a task waiting to be done, your environment is not supporting your wellness and wellbeing!

## The Flourishing Blueprint

When a builder sets about building a house, he works with a blueprint. The blueprint tells him how to lay the foundation and the dimensions of each room. Before work begins, he knows which space goes where, how the plumbing and electrical lines will be laid, and where the doors and windows go. Just as importantly, if the builder gets a request to change materials or a room's dimensions, the blueprint offers an overview of the best way to implement those changes.

To get the most out of The Flourishing Home, consider creating your own blueprint. It's really nothing more than setting goals. Meaningful goals make a tremendous difference. They become a yardstick for measuring your progress. As you reach milestones, you can celebrate each step forward. Your accomplishments can even set you up for future success by opening the door to bigger goals.

Your goals should be SMART: specific, measurable, achievement oriented, realistic, and timely. They should also be thriving goals, ones that move you toward accomplishment rather than merely avoiding failure. They should resonate positively and be in line with personal and family values. Good goals build upon each other and don't conflict with each other.

### Goals

In the world of coaching, questions that trigger strong responses are asked before goals are addressed. The questions include:

- Why now?
- What do you value?
- Why is that important?
- What resources do you have at hand?
- What are your strengths? What are the family's strengths?
- What are the obstacles? Which are real and which are perceived?
- How much time and money can you dedicate?
- What information is needed before you can begin?

Answer these for yourself. You'll end up with touchstones to return to again and again as you draw up your own Flourishing Home blueprint.

To help you reach as many of your goals as possible, write them down. Keep your list in a place where it can be seen often. Make your goals known to other people who will champion your efforts. As you continue reading this book, questions will prompt insight into your goals. Post your answers in a place where you can see them.

A good architect will help you discover your desired changes, build a solid foundation, and set and achieve meaningful, life-enhancing goals. This book will be your architect, your resource, and your inspiration as you create your Flourishing Home. Worksheets, templates and idea sparks will offer straightforward and creative solutions.

---

**Idea Spark: Forward Thinking**

List a single word that defines what each household member would like accomplish during for the next year.

---

## Building a Foundation

- List the people in your home
- List the rooms in your home
- What is the primary purpose of the room?
- What are your eyes drawn to that is positive? Negative?
- What are the areas of stress?

## A Home Mission Statement

A successful business or organization has a mission statement and guiding principles. A mission statement defines a purpose, a reason for being. A good mission statement explains why an organization exists and what it hopes to achieve. It articulates the organization's essential nature, its values, and its work.

Your home can have a mission statement and guiding principles. These should be laid out in a brief paragraph. Periodically review it with your family and have everyone living there agree to its principles. Questions to consider:

- What do we do?

- Why do we do it?
- How do we do it?

Ask everyone to list words, phrases or ideas that come to mind about the home. Allow everyone input without censoring or editing. Look for language and concepts that most individuals agree on.

A good mission statement will be brief and easily understood. The set of statements will be proactive and will motivate family members. It will embody the Flourishing Home's philosophies, goals, and ambitions and mores.

### Idea Spark: Mind Map

Working in a single room, make a list of all the visible objects. Figure out what category each item could be placed into. This creates an inventory of the various things in your home.

## Detective Work

For this, you'll look back at specific areas to find patterns and issues that need to be addressed.

- First check your calendar. What activities run throughout the year?
- Then look at your checkbook to assess your spending habits. What common themes do you find?
- What achievements did you reach in the previous year?
- What issues did you face?

### Idea Spark: Family Symbol

Some properties, like farms, have names that identify the place as much as the address. Create a real or virtual sign for your home. This can look like a family crest, flag or symbol that will incorporate the values, goals, feelings and ideas that are important to you and your family.

CHAPTER TWO

# PRIMES

*T*his chapter provides you with a wickedly simple and free tool that will improve your wellness and wellbeing. This tool can be applied to any living area, work space or property. Best of all, you already have everything you need right at hand.

Primes are cues that prompt you to behave or think in a specific way. If you've ever stuck a gold star on your child's report card to encourage good grades, you've already used this tool. If you've ever visited a doctor's office and seen photos of athletes paired with inspirational sayings, you've already experienced this technique in action. Primes can evoke desired feelings, express values, and help you attain goals.

This tool can be subtle or overt, conscious or unconscious, positive or negative. Primes are everywhere! They include sights, smells, sounds, colors, and textures. They can be computer passwords, screen savers, jewelry, and tattoos. Yup, even tattoos! "Strength" linked on a woman's arm can help her through a difficult divorce or a tiny sun can symbolize a battle won against breast cancer. Most primes are a little less permanent but they are as personal as your life's history.

Research indicates that as much as 80% of our actions are directed by our subconscious reactions to people or signals in our environment. If the primes in our environment work against us, we undercut our goals without even being aware of it! Positive primes, on the other hand, result in positive behaviors or feelings. They can motivate, inspire, aid in goal attainment, improve self-confidence, and trigger desired moods. There is no limit to what positive primes can do or how they can affect your life. When we apply this powerful concept to our home's wellness and wellbeing, voila! A free and wickedly easy tool!

## Positives Primes

Take a minute to look around your home. What primes do you find? What kinds of things hang on the walls? What items are set out for display? What do you smell and hear? Are the primes positive or negative? Revisit your answers to the sidebars you've come across so far.

The questions under Building a Foundation helped you identify positive and negative primes. The Feelings and Values section identified the ones you consider important. The Appreciative Inquiry focused on elements that can be translated into positive primes. The Retrospective questions might have identified recurring themes. The inspiration board might have identified primes you want in your environment.

In this section, we'll look at how existing and new positive primes can help you achieve your goals for your Flourishing Home.

### 1. Positive People Primes

Each of us has an astonishing number of people in our lives. Often when we think about our most personal goals and desires, we consider only how our close friends and immediate family can help, but there's an entire world filled with individuals who touch us in special ways every day. Our coworkers might be our best support for work-related issues. A neighbor we don't see very often might have a lifestyle that is so peaceful or adventurous that it inspires us to reach our own goals. And, of course, our families and friends interact with us in ways that can be surprising, inspiring and exciting!

Support can go far beyond offering advice or sharing a cup of coffee. An individual who makes you feel good just by being who they are is a very positive thing. The subconscious messages you get from individuals can be as diverse as *I love you* to *I love living next to you.* Individually, the smallest kinds of support might not seem monumental. Taken together, however, they are an important part of the Flourishing Home.

Jackie keeps a picture of herself and her son besides her bed. The picture was taken when he was a sweet, cuddly toddler. The son is now in the throes of his teenaged years and sports the know-it-all attitude common to blossoming adulthood. The picture reminds Jackie to be patient. Remembering those tender moments when he was so vulnerable helps her support him as he steps out into the world… still vulnerable, of course, but less inclined to admit it!

Primes relating to specific individuals don't have to be photos. You might hold onto that softball your daughter smacked over the fence during her team's first playoff. A necklace displayed in an open box on a dresser can remind you of a mother or grandmother who has died Although pets aren't people, they are nearly as much a part of the family as humans, so you might keep the collar of a cherished dog hung on your bedpost. Work with what calls to you and you'll fill your home with positive people primes.

## 2. Positive Place Primes

Reminders of specific places can fortify an environment of wellness and wellbeing. Vacation pictures of landscapes and tourist destinations are a popular choice. Pick landscapes and cityscapes for places on your bucket list to encourage you to reach those goals. Photographs of wildlife and weather events can satisfy an ingrained urge to look at nature even if you don't have a pretty view at every window.

Historic architecture, intricate church interiors, close-ups of stained-glass windows from Victorian homes, people from different countries wearing traditional clothing, even the colorized starry landscapes created by NASA's Voyager journey can create peace, encourage a bit of positive daydreaming, trigger goals, and release stress.

**Picture Primes**

Technology provides many creative opportunities to incorporate positive picture primes. Computers, smart phones and other devices open with screensavers, lock screens, and slideshow options. Digital picture frames offer unlimited options. Since digital picture frames also come as refrigerator panels, you can place rotating displays nearly anywhere in your Flourishing Home.

Just as you do with people primes, you can use objects to evoke a specific place. African baskets woven by hand, a vial of beach sand, or colored stones collected during a vacation are simple ways to bring other places into your home. Experiment with dried flowers or plants from a specific region or a piece of Southern pottery. Scatter area rugs from India and Indonesia around your bedroom. With a little creativity and some enjoyable research, you can recreate the entire world inside your Flourishing Home!

### 3. Developmental Primes

Earlier I asked you to look for events that repeat over the days, months or years. The ones that bring you joy will be of two primary types: recurring and evolutionary.

Repeating the same events time after time creates a feeling of comfort and stability. It can be freeing to meet your friends for lunch every Wednesday at the same bistro. You don't have to think about what's on the menu, you know pretty much whether it's going to be crowded, and you aren't going to be surprised by the prices. Because you don't have to think about those details, you're totally tuned into chatting with your friends.

An excellent example of this type of event in the Flourishing Home is the family vacation. Brenda knew that mementos from her family's repeated vacations to Lake George offered a pleasant way to express the joy they felt when they were together. The pictures and objects fostered positive feelings and remind her of the value she places on her family.

Evolutionary events are ones that help you move forward in some way. People who attend a spiritual retreat at a yoga center one year and camp alone in the Appalachian Mountains the next are creating opportunities to stretch beyond their usual boundaries. For my family, vacations have become evolutionary: As our family matured, our vacations became more adventurous. Eight years of family escapades have been captured in pictures. We're even known online as the Adventure Family Five.

### 4. Milestone Primes

Honoring positive passages and milestones in your home can evoke feelings of accomplishment. First pair of dance shoes, first home, first car, first vacation…the list is unlimited. Sacraments, religious rites such as bar/bat mitzvahs, graduations, marriage and other positive milestones can be symbolized through primes.

Anne has put baby shoes from all three of her children on display. She added to the collection by including her daughter's first dance shoes and her son's first soccer cleats. Her husband, the soccer fanatic, keeps a memento from the high school game in which he scored his first triple hat. Reminders of these happy first milestones have become positive primes.

### 5. Words and Symbols as Primes

Certain words can trigger specific feelings or behaviors. Remember that your subconscious mind works like an organic mirror. Rather than reflecting exactly what is in front of it, it reflects the most similar thing stored in your memory. So if you see those frowning ancestors in your home office, you might start to feel judged or unhappy. If you have a screen-saver of a beautiful sunset, your mind might retrieve memories of relaxing at the beach. Words and symbols work exactly the same way.

Sarah's laundry room is also the informal entry to her home. Since she uses it every day, she posted a sign reading @ *home* on the wall opposite the informal entry. The simple phrase reminds her to leave the hustle and bustle of the outside world behind as she enters the sanctuary of her home. When she moves to the kitchen sink, she finds big silver letters that read *Inspire*. Each time she remembers to take a deep breath... and discovers inspiration in her Flourishing Home.

Passwords are ideal trigger primes, especially when you want to encourage a certain behavior. Anne used the word *victory* as her password for the online food journal she was keeping to help her lose weight. A favorite word or personal mantra can trigger a positive feeling or work as a reminder to stay peaceful, balanced and joyful. You can buy individual letters in many colors at the party store. Hang them from the ceiling to create an inspirational word mobile!

Symbols can also be a powerful positive prime. Jane uses a narrow border of tulips as her trigger prime. Her family includes an autistic child, so their journey through life isn't like that of other families. It is, however, a daily adventure! The meaning of the tulip border comes from author Emily Perl Kingsley who wrote about taking a trip to Italy and ending up in Holland instead.

That kind of mix-up forces you to change tactics. You'll need to learn things you never thought about before, and along the way you'll meet new people. Holland might not feel as glamorous as Italy but different doesn't mean lesser. Instead you'll find things Italy doesn't have… and you'll be delighted by every discovery. In the end, of course, you will always pine for Italy. Any dream left unlived will leave you with a sense of longing. But if you remain entangled in that grief, you'll never fully appreciate all that Holland has to offer.

### 6. Sensory Primes

Sensory primes are triggers that work through sound, smell or touch. Wind chimes hung outside entryways can create a peaceful feeling whenever you enter or leave your house. A fragrant candle lit at the end of your workday can help you relax. Even the textures of wood or bamboo, upholstery and bedding can generate comfort. Since they work on a subconscious level all the time, sensory primes are important in the Flourishing Home.

Using the answers you provided, (in chapter one,) for the feelings you want to create in a single room, think about what smells, textures, and sounds represent those feelings. The primes you'll choose for your bedroom will probably be vastly different from the ones you use in your kitchen. While the bedroom is often a retreat, the kitchen is often called the heart of the home. The primes in the kitchen can refuel your spirit while you refuel your body.

### 7. Goal Attainment Primes

All positive primes can help you attain goals. Corrie used her picture primes to promote relaxation. Anne used the trigger word *victory* to help with weight management. Jane used tulips so she could approach raising an autistic child as a wonderful adventure. Positive primes help you achieve your own wellness and wellbeing goals.

Peter Gollwitzer, professor of psychology at New York University, has studied ways to make goal attainment more likely. He found that phrasing things in an "if-then" format can triple a person's chances of attaining a goal. Making an if-then statement helps people stay focused on things they might otherwise skip over. He suggests the following general format for the statement:

---

**If–Then**

Pick something important that you'd like to address. Fill in the gaps in the following statement to create your own positive if-then statement prime:

"When I encounter (a specific situation, thought, person, visual clue, etc.), then I will (behave in a certain way, say a certain thing, think a certain thought) so that I can achieve (the goal)."

---

"When I encounter a specific situation (thought, person, visual clue, etc.), I will do the following thing (behave in a certain way, say a certain thing, think a certain thought) so that I can achieve (the goal)."

This tactic can easily be applied in the Flourishing Home. For example:

*When I see my sneakers in the closet in the morning, I will pack my gym bag for a walk at lunch so I can increase my activity level.*
Prime: sneakers. Behavior: walk.
Goal: increased activity.

*When I log into my bank account to pay bills, I will use my password abundance so I can strengthen my financial wellbeing.*
Prime: password. Behavior: controlled spending.
Goal: maintaining a budget.

*When I smell the lavender candle, I will take a deep breath so I can relax at the end of the day.*
Prime: lavender candle. Behavior: deep breath.
Goal: stress management.

*When I open the pantry door, I will see the measuring cups and re-member the importance of portion sizes so I can achieve my weight loss goals.*
Prime: measuring cups. Behavior: using proper portion sizes.
Goal: weight loss.

Hopefully, your mind is already whirling with good ideas for positive primes you can use. The possibilities are unlimited!

## Negative Primes

A negative prime is anything that makes you react negatively. The two most important categories of negative primes are guilt gifts and family burdens. They include anything you hold onto out of obligation or guilt, or because it's part of your family's heritage. Rather than evoking pleasure, these things create a yucky feeling and are anything but a positive influence on your environment.

While discussing her decor, Karen pointed out several items that evoked a strong negative response. The desk to the right of the entryway, she said, "was my father-in-law's and I hate it." When describing her shelving, which was a focal point in the front room, she explained that the Hummel figurines decorating it had been handed down from her mother. They were not really her style and did not bring her joy.

Once she became mindful of the items' negative effects, we came up with a few minor but significant ideas. She closed the desktop and covered it with a beautiful decorative cloth that created an earthy coziness. Candles of different shapes, sizes and colors placed on top helped her feel warmth and comfort. The figurines were minimized by displaying only one in a less obvious spot. She is even considering selling some of them and using the proceeds to attend a yoga retreat.

A similar type of negative prime is the gift you keep because you don't want to hurt anyone's feelings. During Suzanne's Home Wellness Walkthrough, she described her ideal master bath and dressing area as an inviting, clean space where she could start and end each day. Her vanity was piled with unopened boxes of perfumes, candles and other gift items. They took up half the counter space and held a thin layer of dust. She would never use them because they weren't her style or taste.

If you don't enjoy something, find pleasure in it, utilize it or love it then pass it on, donate it, give it to a friend... but don't keep it around. Not only is it a negative prime, it's clutter! It's amazing how many people keep items that are an obligation and a burden. Often those items enjoy center-stage placement! If you have things that evoke resentment, you have permission to downsize, minimize, lovingly store, donate or toss them!

### Dealing with Negative Primes

- Remove and discard
- Remove and stow away
- Move to a less-visible area
- Donate
- Give it away

OK, I know some of you are thinking *re-gift*. That's up to you. Some etiquette books give the following guidelines: Always rewrap the item, make sure all tags or notes have been removed, never re-gift in the same circle, and don't re-gift if the item looks remotely used. Most importantly, be sure it's something the recipient will enjoy.

## Implementing What You've Learned

Now that you understand primes, revisit each room in your house. What primes already exist in each room? Are they negative or positive? To create positive results, the best ratio is three positive primes for every negative one. For example, the laundry room almost always has a negative prime: piles of laundry! Unfortunately, the piles are a functional constant and can't truly be eliminated. Incorporate more positive primes in this area to offset the negative one. You'll find that the work seems much easier when you're surrounded by positive primes.

After becoming aware of primes, Anne took inventory of her office space. Family pictures dating back to the 1920s and 1930s decorated her shelves. Back then, cameras couldn't enhance the natural light. Anyone who wanted a picture taken had to sit very still for quite some time. If they stopped smiling, their faces would end up blurry. That's why so many of the old pictures we have show people who stare out at us with frozen expressions.

In Anne's case, many of her ancestors looked downright miserable! Even if she had understood the limits of technology, the frowning faces staring down at her every day still would have made her uncomfortable and unhappy. Once she became mindful of how objects can affect feelings, the pictures were lovingly stored away. She surrounded herself with items that symbolize her successes and milestones—artwork by her children, happy family pictures, and the words *peace* and *love*.

This individual started out with some very negative primes in her environment. With only a little effort, she eliminated the negative primes and replaced them with positive ones. Becoming aware of both positive and negative primes can help you take control of your environment, gain insight, and create your best life.

## Inspiration Board, Part Two

Take another look at your inspiration board. What things on your board currently exist in your environment? Which of these things do you want more of? What aspects of the inspiration board are missing in your environment?

Julie realized that her inspiration board had many colorful, whimsical elements such as flowers. It also held plenty of natural elements—greenery and wood. Yet her environment lacked bright colors. Her low-cost solution was to add colorful throw pillows to her family room. She also rearranged the artwork to create more vibrancy. Although she already had plants, she added more to her tabletops.

## Appreciative Inquiry, Part Two

For each answer to the Appreciative Inquiry, brainstorm positive primes that are symbolic or that trigger positive emotions, actions or goal accomplishment for your Flourishing Home.

# CHAPTER THREE

# TUNING INTO TRANSITION POINTS

*R*emember when I said that a Flourishing Home can't make you exercise, lose weight or feel better? I also said the Flourishing Home can make all those things easier to do. In the next several chapters, we'll look at specific areas inside your home that can be modified, adapted or adjusted in quick and easy ways to help you reach those goals. If you dedicate a little effort right now to making these changes, the impact will stay with you long after the work is done.

This chapter is all about to transition points. A transition can be a "period of change from one state or condition to another." Transitions can mark a change in your state of being. We tend to think of transitions in terms of switching jobs, returning to college, moving to a new town, and other life-changing events.

In our everyday lives, though, we undergo transitions month to month, week to week, and even hour by hour. When we prepare to go to work in the morning, we're transitioning out of the home environment into a different activity. When we settle down to sleep in the evening, we transition from being busy to a calm, restful mode. Even going to the kitchen to cook or visiting the shed before mowing the lawn, marks a transition from one focus to another. An important part of building the Flourishing Home is to make these transitions happen smoothly and efficiently.

A transition can also be "a smooth connection between two topics or sections." The Flourishing Home has spaces that connect the different aspects of your life. For example, vacations happen outside the home but are an important part of your mental wellbeing and a way to strengthen family bonds. People who do a little work at home need to be able to keep their work areas separate yet integrated in useful and effective ways.

We'll use different tools and techniques for each space in your home.

Every individual in your family will benefit. The Flourishing Home even provides your guests with a comforting, nurturing experience by creating transitional spaces that focus on them!

## Day by Day

While the tools and tips in this book can help you make big shifts like starting a new career or welcoming a newborn, most readers want and need help with their routine lives. The primary part of the week is spent at work so we should maximize our relaxation time in the evenings and weekends. The best way to do this is to consider the cycle of a typical day.

Your body and mind are programmed by nature to do this. Every living thing is born with a circadian rhythm, a cycle that ebbs and flows according to the time of day. The cycle takes roughly twenty-four hours to run its course. In its simplest form, the circadian rhythm is used by flowers that open in the morning and close up again at night. Birds actively defend their territories by singing in the morning and evening hours then spend the middle of the day looking for food. Their internal clocks have developed over thousands of years. People evolved to take advantage of the daylight hours so we can do all the things we need to survive and thrive.

Along the way, we developed the ability to stay up later and rise earlier. Fires and lanterns gave way to electric lights. Recently we've started using lighted screens on our television sets, computers, and handheld electronics. Although these technologies enhance our lives, they can also throw off our internal clocks. We aren't ready to sleep just because we switch off the light; the transition is sudden and our bodies get confused. It's nothing like the gradual ebb of daylight as the sun goes down. The body is still in active mode...and so is the brain.

Lying in bed can suddenly become a production of *What Should I Worry About Next?* Twenty minutes tick by before your body is ready for sleep. By then you've rehashed seventeen different mistakes from the day, none of which are really worth your time. You've made several mental to-do lists, none of which you'll remember in the morning. You've twitched at every itch, rustled around until the sheets are tangled around your legs, and jolted your partner from his or her own weak grab at rest.

In too many homes, transitions don't happen easily. A poorly lit bathroom doesn't help the mind switch into daytime mode. Too often contractors don't position lights in the bathroom well enough to fully light all the different areas. The shower in particular ends up shadowy and gloomy. Add a curtain or an opaque glass door and you've stuffed yourself into a tiny cave as if you're hiding from a hungry bear. Not the way to start the day!

*The Flourishing Home* will consider several of the most common types of transitions. Since your household and your family members are individuals, you'll have at least a few unique transition points. The tools and tips presented in this chapter will help you enhance your wellness and wellbeing at every step. Ready? Let's transition into a happy, healthy, sexy home!

## The Transition Before the Transition

The Flourishing Home is more than just your house's interior spaces. To gain the maximum benefits, the exterior spaces have to be given the same attention as the living room or kitchen. Even those of you who live in condos or apartments have to consider your outdoor spaces. That's because the process of transitioning into your home environment starts before you even step through the door.

The area you pass through to reach your entryway is a preliminary transition point. Think of this as a space that allows you to prepare for the transition. It's like setting the table before dinner. By arranging plates and silverware around a pretty centerpiece, you're preparing to share a nurturing meal with your family. The same thing happens before you cross the threshold into your home…the exterior space can be arranged so that it prepares you for the comfort of your Flourishing Home.

Common preliminary transition points include your driveway, the sidewalk in front of your home, the garage or carport, a front porch or a side patio. For condos and apartments, preliminary transition points might be an assigned parking spot, the mailbox grouping, the stairwell, an elevator, a porch or recessed front door, or a patio. Each offers opportunities to help you let go of the worries and issues you face at work or with friends.

A driveway or sidewalk might seem unimportant, but for anyone living in a detached home or townhouse, it's the first point of contact with your property. Planting shrubs or placing a line of potted plants along the edges brings natural beauty to these areas. Even driveways and sidewalks with a small border or no grassy border can be enhanced with a stone garden statue or a trio of whimsical butterflies mounted on stakes.

For one man, his preliminary transition point is the driveway. As a father of three young children, he is often met by a ton of toys strewn across the driveway. Before he can even park the car, he has to get out and pick up anything that's in the way. The stress it caused him wasn't terrible but there was a subtle twinge associated with the extra chore. In his case, the children were too young to put away their toys.

The solution was as easy as changing the way he thinks. Now whenever he arrives home to find tiny trucks and Lego bricks strewn across the pavement, he reminds himself how important it is for kids to play outside. As long as they're in the driveway and the yard, they're safe. Instead of thinking about the extra chore, he pictures how much fun the kids have constructing make-believe worlds with their dolls and action figures. These images counteract the stress he might otherwise feel.

Sometimes the approach to a home can be enhanced by changes to the home's interior. Sophie, a young professional who purchased a townhouse, wanted to support her wellness by minimizing the stress of being a night nurse. The companionship of her pets was a big part of this whenever she was in the house. She installed a cat perch under the window that overlooked her reserved parking space. Now she's welcomed home by the faces of her two cats peering through the glass!

Sophie was also soothed by nature so she purchased a few outdoor planters and placed them beside the entry. Despite the lack of lawn or garden space, she created the natural elements she values so highly in her preliminary transition point. Her simple solution helped her begin to relax and unwind before she even stepped inside.

Your approach to your home's preliminary transition points will be as unique as your needs. Seasonal flags hung on the mailbox can call to you long before you turn up the driveway. Hedges that screen you from traffic or from your neighbors can provide a sense of privacy before you're inside. A tall tree or an arbor over the drive can shelter you from sun or rain while you gather your things from the car. Even an assigned parking space can be spruced up now and then with a chalk picture drawn on the asphalt.

A preliminary transition point for my family occurs when our garage door goes up. As I pull the car inside, I am face to face with a wall of artwork my children created over the last fifteen years. One finger painting titled *This is Mom* shows my happy face hovering over a pair of feet with no body in between. A note my son wrote to his father and school poster projects have been tacked to the wall. Many of the items are faded and wrinkled, but each one reflects happy moments. Every time we arrive home, we are tangibly reminded of our flourishing family life!

Renters and condo owners can use many of the same things homeowners might have at their doorways. A set of wind chimes can always be counted on for a beautiful interlude. Metal artwork intended for garden fences can just as easily decorate a front door. The bars of a security door can be woven with wide strips of ribbon in colors that match the season.

No matter where you live, you can incorporate decorative or funny welcome mats and seasonal door hangers. A parson's table decorated with a single item alongside a narrow chair or stool creates a welcoming tone. A pinwheel staked by the door can provide whimsy and color. Your options are limited only by your imagination…and your imagination is limitless!

---

### Idea Spark: First Impressions

Take a look at your home's exterior and locate the preliminary transition points. What colors, shapes and objects are there? What are your eyes drawn to? Is it positive or negative? How does each item or element reflect you? Do you want to set your home apart from others?

---

## The First Step

Once you cross any of your home's thresholds, you are standing in the entry area. This area is the portal from the chaos of the larger world back into your sanctuary. It's also the portal from your personal universe back to the outside world. The area might be the front porch of your home, a garage off the side, or even the patio at the rear of the house. No matter where the space is located, the Flourishing Home has entry areas that make the transition as soothing and uplifting as possible. These spaces benefit the wellness and wellbeing of every family member and visitor.

Just look at the time and money invested in designing the entryways of spas and high-end restaurants. Both businesses nourish the mind, body and spirit. Both use background music, color and textures to create a feeling of being wrapped in comfort and luxury. We can take lessons from these establishments to generate a personalized and genuinely comforting experience in the Flourishing Home.

One of the most important lessons is to think about how each of the senses can be stimulated. Wind chimes or a small waterfall can soothe through sound. Fragrant potted plants or a drop of vanilla on a light bulb can fill the space with a gentle scent. A thick throw rug or a heavy brass doorknob can provide a sense of timeless luxury while a mural or colorful piece of art offers a lively view.

## Formal Entry Transition Points

The characteristics of formal transition points are different from those of informal ones. Formal transition points often welcome friends, acquaintances and newcomers. While the informal entry is often casual, the formal entry sets the symbolic tone. If arranged properly, the formal entry can send a message about the home.

Jill, for example, resisted using the kind of furniture and decor usually found in a formal entry area. Instead she selected highly personal objects. Everyone who enters immediately gets to know something about her or her family. The message of her family theme is clear: the envi-

### Sensory Extras

Examine the lighting at your entry points. The most soothing is usually ambient light like a table lamp mixed with an overhead fixture for function. Consider adding a small lamp to your entry area. If that's not the right fit, try a dimmer switch on the overhead light.

Next consider the textures. Would adding a cushy rug help absorb sound? Can you apply a textured paint to the walls to create the feeling that you are moving into a soft, comforting space? You might also upgrade the hardware on the doors to help you feel that your home is secure.

Now consider all the other things that stimulate your senses. Hang a tiny set of bells on the doorknob for a bright, joyful welcome. Use an automatic air freshener filled with your favorite scent in this space. Pot your favorite herb and pinch off a leaf whenever you need a boost. It's your home...let it help you flourish!

ronment people are moving into is warm, friendly, unpretentious, inviting, and most of all, unique. Her formal entry therefore represents her values and sets the theme for her home.

Historical, religious, and cultural symbols or primes are found in many formal entries. A family might utilize the history of its state or country to reflect an important part of who they are. Antique farm tools or items salvaged from old train yards can reflect the importance of agriculture or the rail in a certain region. A collection of cornhusk dolls from the Southern Appalachian Mountains might be tucked into a cradle carved in Williamsburg, Virginia, to reflect both spouses' heritages.

Spiritual or religious icons frequently appear in entryways. The mezuzah, for example, is a constant reminder of God's presence and His commandments. Every time you pass through, you touch the mezuzah, then kiss your fingers to express love and respect for God. Crosses and crucifixes are sometimes found in the entryways of Christian homes. Talismans such as the Khamsa or Hasma symbols ward off evil eyes. Catholics might display icons or pictures of the Virgin Mary.

Cultural items are also commonly used. Ugly jugs, pottery with bizarre faces crafted on their sides, are old Southern icons still used today as coffee mugs, flower vases and whimsical decorations. African mud clothes or Indonesian tapestries might hang in an entryway to honor the culture of an adopted child. A pair of crossed arrows is a symbol of friendship in some Native American tribes and might hang anywhere in the entryway area.

Don't forget how colors can convey your family theme. One of my clients wanted her home to radiate joy. After figuring out exactly which rooms were visible from her entry area, Carol painted each space a different bright color. Her dining room ended up with yellow stripes! A border, painted molding, or wall stickers available in everything from classic and sophisticated shapes to animals and plants can add a splash of color and visual interest to your Flourishing Home.

---

**Formal Introduction**

Go to your formal entry area. Starting at the outermost point, move through the threshold and into the middle of the space. Now look around.

- What positive primes are there now?
- What would you like to add?
- Do you have a family icon or symbol that can be incorporated here?

---

Textures also make a big difference. Jill used warm earth tones to make visitors feel welcome. To this she might add textures like wheatgrass wallpaper, a Berber carpet as thick and soft as a layer of moss, a chandelier or lampshade hung with quartz crystals, a row of candles in cedar holders… the possibilities are endless. Taken together, the details create an entryway that hugs your friends as warmly as you do!

## Informal Entry Transition Points

Common informal entry areas include mud rooms, laundry rooms, and the garage. Other informal entryways include a rear or side door to the house. Rather than lead you into a small space that is dedicated to a specific use like the laundry area, the rear and side entryways often dump you directly into the living room or kitchen. These can make you work a little harder to set up a good transition zone. Don't worry; I have some great ideas for them, too!

Your overall approach will be the same as your approach to the formal transition areas: use color, textures, sound, light and symbols to create a certain feeling. Rather than focusing on how you want your guests to feel, this time it's all about you! If your informal transition area is also a work space, this can be a challenge. After my family goes through the garage, we step into the laundry room.

**Who Needs What?**

It's important to ask everyone who lives in the home to speak up about their needs and desires. One person's joy can cause another person stress. Teenagers are often happy to leave their clean laundry piled up in the corner. That usually creates stress for at least one adult. The answer could be to move all the clean clothes onto the bed. The clothes have to be put away or hung up before the kids go to sleep. What are the wants and needs of the people in your home? How can those needs and desires be met while honoring the needs and desires of others? Find the solution and you'll be a big step closer to a Flourishing Home.

I love this room. It's filled with whimsical, colorful posters with titles like *How to Really Love a Child* and *Dedication to Dogs,* artwork created by my kids, pictures of our extended family, and funny family photos of us in our Christmas PJs. Still, the laundry room is also a functional hub (see the next chapter for more on Hubs) and can therefore cause stress. Arriving home after a day at work, we're often met by loads of laundry waiting to be done, wet clothes waiting to be transferred from the washer to the dryer, one pile waiting to be folded, another waiting for the iron, and piles that haven't been put away. My husband refers to it as instant mayhem!

In a world of unlimited budgets and time, the answer would be easy: Remodel and redesign until the area is both functional and beautiful. However, budgets and time are real factors all of us must balance. The answer our family voted for was to find a laundry genie who would grant our every wish. We're still waiting. In the meantime, we're all making a greater effort to pitch in together and get things done more quickly.

---

**Positivity Ratio**

In a previous chapter, I talked about the ratio of positive to negative feedback. A ratio of 3 positive feedback events to 1 negative feedback event creates a positive relationship. Anything under 3 to 1 spells danger.

Walk through the threshold into your informal transition area. What are your eyes immediately drawn to? Is it positive? If you can't change the negative aspect, what three things can you adjust to counteract that negative?

---

## Transitioning into Wellness and Wellbeing

Your informal transition points are truly important to your wellness and wellbeing. Susan is a busy single mother of two kids. She's also a teacher. Every weekday morning she must get her children ready for school, make breakfast, pack up the children's homework, prepare their lunches, select the proper outerwear for that day's weather, and get the kids out the door. In what little time is left, she has to get herself ready for work. Phew! I'm already tired just hearing about it!

Anyone with school-age children can probably relate. Mornings can be a daunting, frustrating and stressful time because a lot needs to happen in a short period of time. In her pre-interview, Susan said she wanted efficient storage space that would simplify her life and create a more calming, peaceful home environment. She has two main entryways: the front door and the door from the garage into the laundry room. Her children leave and return through the front door. She leaves and returns through the laundry room. The front door is a formal transition point, used by family, friends and visitors, while the other is an informal transition point used mainly by the family.

Her goals were to simplify and decrease her stress so she could enjoy more time with her children as well as practice yoga and meditation. But the transition points were working against her. Her work-to-home transition area landed her smack in the middle of the laundry room chaos. It was difficult to shift out of work mode when dirty clothes, cleaning supplies, a vacuum cleaner and other chore reminders greeted her.

After only a few minor tweaks, she reaped a big dividend. The coat closet in that area got a quick overhaul. The seldom-used carpet cleaner was stored away and all the gift-wrapping supplies were moved to the top shelf. After straightening up the laundry room and utilizing colors, textures, symbols and positive primes, she felt a completely different response whenever she came home at the end of the day.

When we looked at the children's transition point, the formal entryway, we focused on the two closets in that area. Each child was assigned one of the closets. The interiors were set up so that one part was dedicated to the outerwear they might need depending on the weather. Mittens, rain gear, snow gear and coats are ready to go, so there's no more running around trying to find the umbrella. There's also less shouting and less stress.

When the children return from school, all their gear and backpacks go right into the closet. No more nagging to put away school stuff! Of course, any new habit takes

### Issues with Entryways

Entryways are often dumping grounds. A bench, shelf or table can offer a place to put things other than on the floor. A shelf can have small baskets for different people while a bench can provide storage under the seating area. Revisit the system every once in a while as seasons change and kids grow older.

time and effort to create. By consistently reminding the kids to use the new transition point, these simple steps allowed the evenings to become calm, happy hours filled with after-school activities, homework, meals, and more time to relax. Susan ended up with less stress, more positive interactions with her children, and more time for the things she enjoys. If that doesn't improve her wellness and wellbeing, I don't know what will!

## Routine Transitions

If you were born before 1998, I'll bet you can remember Mr. Rogers singing "It's a beautiful day in the neighborhood." After walking through the door (entry transition point), he put on his red sweater, sat on a bench, removed his dress shoes and put on his sneakers. By the time the song ended, he'd transitioned from the outside world into the world of his home.

He'd also transitioned from daily life into his evening routine. This second kind of transition—what we'll call a routine transition point—includes moving from rest into the day's activities, from home life into the work world, out of the day's activities and into relaxation mode, and from relaxation to sleep. Every one of these routine transition points can support your wellness and wellbeing.

Frequently these routine transition points take up a very small amount of space. They typically include closets and bathrooms. They could be as simple as a narrow built-in shelving unit or a storage box. Some of them might not be any larger than Mr. Roger's bench! Believe it or not, though, these tiny areas can enhance your life in big ways. Often they're critical for your wellness.

For example, when we get up in the morning, most of us use the bathroom and brush our teeth. Good oral health reduces the risk of gum disease. Plaque bacteria in the bloodstream can increase the risk of heart disease and

**Bath Area Wellness and Wellbeing**

- Get rid of old medicine and old makeup.
- The closet, that other common transition point, can also support our wellness. Many of us want to get more exercise. Moving our bodies can give us more strength, increase our mental and physical energy, and clear away stress. The closet should be organized so that exercise clothes are ready to go. When you can easily grab your equipment, you'll have more time to work out because you'll waste less time thinking about how to do it! A bathroom with soap, hair care products, makeup and other essentials, neatly organized, can minimize the time spent washing up after a workout...so that's one less excuse for not exercising!

Both these transition points can also support our wellbeing. Sarah, a single professional, wrote a personal message on her bathroom mirror so she could begin each day with a positive attitude. Anne has placed the affirmation *Begin each new day thankful for another day of loving* in her closet where she'll see it every morning. Every night my daughter highlights whatever she's looking forward to the next day on a white board alongside personal affirmations.

stroke. The same bacteria can cause lung infections or aggravate existing lung conditions. Pregnant women with gum disease are at higher risk of delivering pre-term, low birth weight babies. Having the best tools on hand for dental hygiene is therefore a no-brainer!

# Flip the Switch

*Your one week of vacation is finally here! You've arrived, unpacked, and are ready to enjoy some down time, yet your brain is still in work mode. After a day or two you're finally relaxing... aah. Midway through the vacation you realize your return to the real world is looming. You switch back into work mode long before you've hit the road. A week's break amounts to a day or two midweek!*

*Sometimes it takes days to transition into, or out of, our multiple roles. We miss much-needed opportunities to relax, spend quality time with our families, or recharge our spiritual sides. This difficulty also affects the transitions we make in our daily roles. Whether you're on vacation or are visiting your personal time-out zone, mental chatter robs you of many things: time to refuel and indulge in self care, the ability to engage in an activity to the point of flow, and nourish positive relationships. You're missing out on all the aspects of a Flourishing Home that enhance wellness and wellbeing.*

**Your Closet Secrets**

- Are you holding on to clothing you'll never wear again? Consider whether you're clinging to some aspect of your old self, and whether it's time to let that go.
- What colors dominate? Which pieces do you feel fantastic in?
- Why?
- What's your favorite outfit? How is it cut, how does it fit, and where do you wear it? Be sure to record any light bulb insights you have!

*Go back to David, the father who pulls into a driveway filled with toys. This physical transition point also marks his transition into a different role. As the car turns in, he transitions out of work mode and into the role of father, husband and friend. If he arrives home unaware that he's transitioning, he stays in work mode. He grudgingly mutters hello to his children, trudges through the house, and deposits himself in his office to catch up on email.*

With only a slight shift in awareness, David can make his return home much more positive. When he pulls into his driveway (a physical preliminary transition point), he spots the happy flag hanging from the mailbox. *If I see this flag*, he thinks, *I know I'm home and can relax.* This positive prime helps shift his mindset. He is aware that he has returned home (a physical transition) and that he is again a father, husband and friend (role transition). He greets his children with a smile and asks about their days. The different mindset fosters positive relationships before he even enters the house.

*In our home, the roles of wife and parent are often out of balance. As a wife, I am a best friend, intimate secret keeper, and hopefully still have the spark that initiated the relationship. As a parent and a partner in raising a family, I am responsible for various family needs. Sometimes the partner role dominates and the wife role is put on the back burner. The tasks and obligations of daily life can overshadow the role of BFF.*

*The kicker is that we function best when we dedicate time to our roles as husband and wife. The intimate connection that brought us together is strengthened in these moments, and our whole family benefits. Your relationship might be with an unmarried domestic partner, a same-sex individual, or a blended family with children from different partners. No matter your situation, set aside time to interact as a couple to enhance the bond you both value so highly.*

**Points of Transition Versus Transition Points**

- What roles do you have?
- How can becoming mindful of your roles create positive benefits?
- How can your Flourishing Home affect each role?
- What roles do the different people living in your home have?

*Adults are often aware of the different roles we play from vice president of a large corporation to parent volunteer, spouse, friend, and so on. For a child or teenager, the transition from home to school, school to home, into homework mode or out of extracurricular activities can be a bit tricky. Once their work day (school) is over, it can be hard to gear up into homework mode. Not to worry; the Flourishing Home can help!*

**Family Transitions**

- What kinds of family transitions happen in your household?
- What truly works for you and the rest of the family?
- What new things do you want to try?

*Barb helped her children transition from school to home by allowing them a small break before they did any homework. Her husband, on the other hand, preferred that the children transition from school to homework right away. The beauty of the Flourishing Home is that what works best for them is unique to them. In this case, doing homework right away left the rest of the evening open for play. A space in the kitchen became an efficient workspace where they could eat a snack while they completed the day's assignments.*

## Healthy, Happy Routine Transitions

Be aware of your home's transition points. Consider how each transition point supports your wellness and wellbeing. Positive primes are great tools for these areas!

*Even inside our homes, we transition into and out of different roles many times a day. By being mindful of our roles, we can set up our homes to support our wellness and wellbeing. When a functional hub runs smoothly, the work role at home takes less time. If a parental role is less stressful, the intimate relationship role can grow deeper. If the spirit is refueled, the possibilities are limitless! By creating a Flourishing Home, you can transition between your life roles in a way that generates more happiness and health.*

**Bathroom Scale**

Love it or hate it, research gathered from multiple long-term studies found that people who lost weight and kept the weight off weighed themselves regularly...yup, as in daily. Yikes! If weight loss and maintenance is your goal, make sure your scale is accurate. Put an item with a known weight on the scale. If the item weighs accurately, your scale is accurate. Most scales have an adjustment button or bar.

How you handle routine transitions can impact your happiness and health. Our family transitions into the evening by lighting an aromatic candle. The soothing aroma and soft flicker of light helps us focus on each other and our relationships. For many people, the biggest end-of-day transition occurs when retiring for the evening. Again, most people will brush their teeth and change into pajamas...so we're back to the bathroom and the closet.

Some individuals take time to reflect or pray. You might sit down with a journal, think back on what you accomplished, or simply close your eyes long enough to let go of all your worries. Usually people wait until after they've finished up in the bathroom. Whether you sit on a chair near the bed or snuggle under the covers, take a moment to put the day to rest. You'll transition peacefully into a good night's sleep.

# CHAPTER FOUR

# FLOURISHING HOME HUBS

Seeking Home Hub Manager.
Responsibilities include:
Laundry Genie
Personal Assistant
Full Time Housekeeper
Location: Home hub
Start: Immediately!

*W*hile we're creating a Flourishing Home that will be a sanctuary and a retreat, the reality is that bills need to be paid, clothes needs to washed, meals need to be cooked, projects need to be started, homework needs to be finished…you get the idea. To reduce stress, maximize your efficiency, and give you more time to enjoy pleasurable activities, your home must increase your productivity. These tasks are best managed in a hub, a centralized location where specific activities take place.

The Flourishing Home has clearly defined areas dedicated to different activities. The contractors who built your home probably designed one of these hubs for you already: the laundry area. If you have a garage, you've probably already designated that as the home repair hub. Building the rest of the hubs is up to you and your family.

Hubs are critical to the Flourishing Home. Think about what happens when you don't have a bill paying hub. Bills arrive and are opened while you prepare dinner. They sit on the dining room table until you transfer them to the sideboard or perhaps leave them by the phone. Eventually they end up beside the computer. When you finally have a few minutes, you fetch your checkbook from the bedroom and record each payment as it's made.

A miniature disaster is just waiting to happen. Envelopes and payment slips can be misplaced at half a dozen points. Due dates creep up unnoticed, leaving you with no choice but to charge the payment on the day it's due…along with a hefty phone or credit card service fee. And since you're paying bills when you have a moment here and there, you miss the opportunity to track your financial wellness with a more formal system.

This important task needs a command central hub. The area you designate for bill paying should have a file folder for receipts you want to keep, a calculator, access to the internet if you pay bills online, your checkbook or a debit card register to track payments, a folder for copies of bills you want to keep, a shredder for anything you need to destroy, and a recycle box for old papers. With everything at your fingertips, the process will take less time, run more smoothly, and be less stressful. Imagine…paying bills can be *less* stressful!

Remember one key point: a hub doesn't have to be a single-use area. Your command central hub might be set up on the same desk as your computer. That way you can access your work calendar, review email invitations from friends, bank online, and track your monthly expenditures in the same place. A file box, a pen, a calculator and some scratch paper are really all you need at the computer desk. With the right tools and little space, you'll create an efficient command central hub.

## Types of Hubs

The Flourishing Home has many types of hubs. Functional hubs (like your command central) handle the necessities of life…bill paying, scheduling vacations, tracking doctor's appointments, and keeping your schedule synced with your spouse's. Hobby hubs provide a centralized area for fun activities. Depending on your hobby, the hub might be a craft table in the living room, a sewing box tucked into a corner, or an entire room devoted to painting. An information hub is the nerve center of the home's organization. These tasks include everything from lists of daily chores, large renovations, special projects, home maintenance and the like.

Getting each of these hubs to work smoothly will support your happiness and health. Then your inner goddess or god can appear more often. Personally, I like her more than the anxious, we-need-to-get-this-done persona. Functional, hobby and information hubs serve both work and play, and are the muscles that keep your home working. You'll find plenty of idea sparks and tips in this chapter. Remember that the most important tools and tactics are the ones that work for you!

## 1. Functional Hubs

Functional hubs have a special purpose or a well-defined task. Generally they're designed to be practical and useful. The more smoothly your functional hubs work, the more time you have for pleasurable activities. Kitchens, mudrooms, laundry areas and garages with separate spots for car maintenance and home projects are typical examples. Having the best tools and tactics at hand will help you become more positive, powerful and productive.

### Discover Your Hubs

- Which activities in your home need a space dedicated to them?
- Break these activities down into functional, hobby, and informational categories.
- For each activity, ask yourself what's working well in the space you've already dedicated to it?
- What keeps each activity from working optimally?

## 2. Hobby Hubs

While functional hubs help chores get done more quickly, hobby hubs are dedicated to pleasurable activities. Craft tables, carpentry workrooms, hobby benches, or any other area set up to support an enjoyable pastime is a hobby hub. In smaller houses and apartments, a hobby hub might appear every evening on the same table where the family eats. In a detached home, the garage can be a functional hub for home repair projects as well as a hobby hub for rebuilding cars. The shed might hold lawn maintenance equipment as well as a potting shelf for people who find gardening relaxing.

Sometimes it makes sense for areas to overlap. At other times, hubs need to be confined to specific areas. Carol's pleasure activities included being an active class mom and Girl Scout coordinator along with DIY home improvement projects. Her strengths included the ability to jump into remodeling projects like redesigning the downstairs bathroom from the floor to the tiling.

The areas she'd remodeled gave her the most satisfaction. For her, it was 3-D artwork. She enjoyed planning her children's birthday parties as well as coordinating her daughter's Girl Scout troop activities. These events gave her a sense of pride, accomplishment and joy. Still, having so many unfinished projects going at once was stressful. During our walkthrough, she frequently said she felt overwhelmed by all her projects.

---

### Idea Spark: The Label is Your Best Friend

Ah, the label. It's just a little strip of paper but it's worth its weight in organizational gold! My husband teases me because I have a labeled container for everything. Sometimes I would like to box, label and stow my emotional struggles! Labels truly help everyone find, retrieve and return the stuff that is necessary for our active lives. The biggest plus at our home is that the labels help our children take a bigger part in maintaining the different hubs. Where would labels help you?

---

The reason was immediately apparent: Her hobbies and the supplies needed to accomplish the different tasks had taken over the entire house. Rather than reminding her of how great she would feel while engaged in each activity, the hobbies had invaded spaces where they clearly didn't belong. One of the holding spots for project supplies was the master bedroom. Not part of the master bedroom, but the entire room! Party hats, bath tiles, tablecloths and hardware were piled in every corner.

Together we designed specific hubs for each type of activity. First we located areas that were the right size to hold the supplies and were conveniently located according to the activity. Consolidating the supplies made the activities more efficient. With everything neatly organized in its own space, Carol was finally able to use the other areas of her home for real relaxation.

### 3. Informational Hubs

The last category, informational hubs, can range from an overflowing to-do basket to a room that holds the home office. This kind of hub should be given a high priority in your Flourishing Home. It's so important, in fact, that if you can accomplish only one thing after reading this entire book, this is it: Set up a command central.

Remember that saying, your home is your castle? Well, a castle is a big place with lots of activity behind the scenes. Butlers and maids, liverymen and chauffeurs, gardeners and cooks are mustered every day to keep the place maintained and well ordered. Although your household might not be as big, keeping it running smoothly can make you feel that you're managing a castle! A Flourishing Home has a command central that keeps everything on schedule. Think of it as the house's CPU. School and sports schedules, grocery lists, to-do notes, calendars, reminders and upcoming invitations are all commonly found at a family's command center.

The space can be as small or as large as you like. A single bulletin board, a portion of the kitchen counter, a compact roll-top desk, a file box or a folding tray table can all serve as an informational hub. If you're single or don't yet have kids, your information hubs might all be at your computer desk. Growing families and people who work out of their homes need a more formal area dedicated to a single information or command hub.

---

### Idea Spark: Broadcast the System

Whenever you set up a system, train everyone in your household to use it. Then keep using it! New behaviors can take as long as three months to become habits. Don't give in or give up. Your household's system is worth the time it takes to teach everyone and then enforce its use. The key is to make sure everyone is on the same page. It's easy to grow frustrated with family members, but if they don't know how to use the system, even the best system won't work. Do you have a system that works for everyone?"

---

No matter what your Flourishing Home needs, remember that informational hubs can be located in untraditional spaces. Jane uses the butler's pantry that connects her kitchen with her dining room as her office. Upper and lower cabinets, a wine storage unit, and a small work surface traditionally staged the evening's entertainment. It's an ideal spot for a family hub. Her computer is readily accessible while she tends to her family's needs and the cabinets give her separate areas for functional and information hubs.

The lack of space, however, presented some challenges. A few simple adjustments were all she needed. The wine cubbies were repurposed to hold bills, outgoing mail, pens, notepads and other supplies she needed on hand. Simple, inexpensive desktop accessories like file holders and pencil boxes were suggested to organize each hub's paperwork and accessories. Soon this area achieved the potential Jane had envisioned and became a humming command central.

**Creating Space**

With all the information available online, rethink the need for phone books and user's manuals. Phone numbers and addresses can be found in seconds on the internet. Most manuals are accessible these days in PDF to reduce manufacturer's costs and paper waste. Take advantage of electronic sources and clear out all that paper you only use once in a while!

The adaptations each hub can have are as individual as the people who use the hubs. Laptops are often used as an individual's primary computer but a separate unit for the household can easily be set up in an unused kitchen cabinet. A slim monitor mounted to the wall leaves the counter free for a keyboard that can be tucked sideways into a cabinet when it isn't in use. While the computer tracks schedules and budgets, a small white board allows the family to leave more immediate notes and reminders for each other. With hubs, a little creativity goes a long way!

## Thinking about Hubs

Becoming mindful of your home's different types of hubs can be powerful. Diane, a mother of three active school-aged children, wanted to "get on top of things... and get organized." Her desire to spend more time outdoors and to volunteer in a more hands-on manner was blocked at every turn by her home's environment. She felt scattered, unable to move forward, and unclear how to make any headway.

As we explored her family's foundation, it became clear that the children's interests were given top priority. Both parents provided wonderful support for their academic pursuits and intellectual curiosity. A variety of extracurricular activities were also encouraged. Books, creative projects, music sheets and electronic experiments had been set up all over the house.

The home's administrative chores were also scattered in different areas. Pieces of to-do lists, bills, maintenance projects and family schedules cropped up everywhere. The end result was a somewhat chaotic environment that left Diane feeling overwhelmed. Three children with three sets of school responsibilities times three sets of interests plus normal household needs equaled chaos!

We tackled the chaos with an orderly process. First we took inventory of the family's activities. Each activity was categorized as functional, hobby or informational. Then we determined how much space would be needed for each of the hubs. We walked through the house again and listed all the areas available for hubs. We also defined the areas where each activity currently took place.

That last step alone provided a great deal of clarity. It revealed how inefficient the current layout was and immediately made a case for consolidation and separation. The first step, then, was to set up command central. A buffet in the kitchen's eating area with all its drawers provided a perfect place. The supplies were easily accessible and everything could be quickly stored away when it was time for a meal.

We then set up hobby hubs and homework hubs for each of her children. We defined what would be needed for each. A shelving unit for each child was taken from other areas of the house and moved into the formal dining room. This room became the homework hub. The room was directly off both the family room and the kitchen, so an adult would always be close by whenever help was needed.

At my house, command central comes in the form of magnetic chalkboards onto which multiple schedules are attached. Since Diane's tastes gravitated toward a clean, modern style, those kinds of tools would have created stress. Her solutions and tactics were therefore different from ours. This goes back to what I love about working with my clients. Ultimately, the solutions that work for your home are completely your own!

## The Trouble with Hubs

Drum roll, please. The number one issue with hubs is...clutter and disorganization. Either one by itself creates stress. Mix the two and you've got a wrecking ball loose in your home!

Over years of training, coaching and counseling, I've heard time and time again:

- *If only I could get organized...*
- *If only I didn't feel so overwhelmed...*
- *If only I could catch up...*

Then I could exercise/relax/do the things I love!

In addition to robbing you of time, clutter is a horde of termites eating away at your walls. It drains you of energy, keeps you tied to the past, and makes you mentally and physically lethargic. It's such an important concept that Feng Shui, an ancient design system, dedicates an entire philosophy to clutter!

A cluttered environment limits your capability to focus and process information. It's flat-out distracting. It competes with the attention you might otherwise dedicate to your children or spouses, your hobbies and your life. You might be able to ignore it for a short time but it continuously chews away at your Flourishing Home. You might not feel the frustration, lethargy and distraction all the time but for most people the anxiety ranges from noticeable to screaming!

One of the few studies on clutter measured how the body and the brain respond to organized and disorganized stimuli. It concluded that clearing clutter from your home and work environments will decrease irritation, increase productivity, and allow you to process information better. There are even anecdotes about people who lost weight because they got rid of their clutter!

---

### Idea Spark: Stuff in Waiting

Let's face it, life is busy so we can't always attend to every detail right away. Set up a reception area, like a basket or a bench, where similar items can gather. Place a basket at the bottom of the steps for shoes that need to go upstairs, set up a catch-all folder for bills that need to be filed, or use a big tub to store random toys in the TV room. When you have a few minutes, you can attend to all the items at the same time.

---

Before going any further, let's be clear: we aren't talking about hoarding. Hoarding is a whole different ballgame that's being studied by experts, and it requires an entirely different kind of intervention. Since the continuum of clutter, disorganization and hoarding is still fuzzy, you might wonder where the line is between each level. Since we can't really define that line, let's assume we're only talking about too much stuff.

**A Hoarding Scale**

If you're concerned that someone's simple residential clutter might actually be hoarding, help is available through the Institute for Challenging Disorganization website.

So what is clutter? While many books tackle organization, one person's clutter can be another person's treasure! I created a straightforward definition to help Flourishing Home clients. The dictionary definition includes words like *confused, unwanted, interference,* and *disorderly.* The concept pinpoints the feeling that there's just too much stuff in too small a space. Even if you lived in that castle, you would still have to deal with clutter!

Clutter can be characterized as items that:

- You do not need
- You do not love
- Do not bring you joy
- Are disorganized
- Cause problems in the family
- Make you feel embarrassed
- Are not welcoming

For the rest of your Flourishing Home, try open-topped baskets to group items you use often. Inexpensive wicker or canvas drawers can be added to almost any bookshelf. Tin containers made to hold dry food items can be repurposed as storage containers that provide a perfect accent amid rustic décor. If you're not sure about using a particular kind of container, just try one in the space you're organizing. You'll quickly figure out if you like it!

**Love the OC**

In this case, the OC is the opaque container. Group and store visual chaos inside opaque containers such as plastic tubs. Now, I'm not a fan of using this solution in high-visibility areas like the family room. The containers tend to be too utilitarian to truly work inside most homes. The one exception is a child's room where colorful OCs might be the perfect solution!

# Defining Clutter

Determining what is and what isn't clutter is a highly subjective and personal process. My daughter's penguin collection, for example, contains roughly fifty stuffed animals, figurines and papier-mâché penguins ranging in size from a couple of inches to a couple of feet tall. To me, that feels like clutter. For her, the collection is beloved. It brings her joy, it generates a sense of pride, and it certainly doesn't cause problems in the family.

Remember Susan from the chapter on primes? Her bedroom's dressing area had piles of unused gifts. She didn't need them, she didn't love them, and they didn't bring her joy. She hadn't used any of them in the previous year. Her pile of unused gifts were negative primes that also qualified as clutter. She didn't like them but there they were, taking up valuable space and draining her energy every time she changed her clothes!

Once you've determined that clutter does indeed exist inside your home, it's important to define the kind of clutter you're looking at. Once you understand the different types, you'll immediately know which set of tools and tactics to bring to bear on each pile. The three types are primary clutter, visual clutter, and invisible clutter.

## 1. Primary Clutter

Primary clutter is basic. It boils down to one concept: too much stuff!

Over the years, I've been in homes where the cabinets are filled with plastic beverage cups from sports games, Broadway shows, music concerts, little league teams, employers, national banks, the local used car lot, the cell phone company, the cable TV provider, the big-box store, and so on...and so on! This kind of stuff couldn't have been used more than a few times a year yet there they were, tumbling out of closets and cabinets whenever a door was opened, overflowing from different drawers, and generally making a nuisance of themselves.

Primary clutter takes all kinds of forms. Shoes that are too worn to wear, a collection of graphic t-shirts, house plants too numerous to properly tend, and that stack of records left over from the '80s all qualify. I know, some of that stuff you might actually need or want. But where do you draw the line? Three simple questions can help you decide whether an item should be kept or tossed.

Have I used it sometime in the last year? Will I need to use it sometime in the coming year? A couple that wants to have more children will keep a baby stroller; a single woman who hires a teenager to cut the lawn doesn't need that mower anytime soon.

*Do I have another one that is newer or simply works better? Should I really keep multiples of the same item?*

As you might imagine, I've helped people from all walks of life get their homes in order. One of my most memorable experiences was with two teenagers who'd lost their mother to cancer. I was asked to help them create soothing spaces in which they could heal and entertain friends. Most of all, the space had to nurture the girls' needs.

Before going into their rooms, we spoke at great length about their personal interests, likes, personalities, color preferences and dislikes...all the aspects of a solid foundation. While we talked, I shared my definition of clutter. It helped both girls decide what they truly valued and what was actually clutter. It was as if they'd been given permission to get rid of things. In only a few hours, their environments felt lighter and more positive. Decluttering was a critical first step toward creating bedrooms that were truly healing spaces.

**Share the Definition**

The working definition of clutter is often helpful for children and adults alike. Especially with children, understanding clutter can invite everyone to be part of the solution. By finding things in their rooms that they no longer need or want, they approach change in a non-threatening way. The experience becomes positive and empowering!

## 2. Visual Clutter

The second type of clutter is visual. It often appears in areas where the right amount of things are located in the right space but their placement is wrong. The typical laundry room is a perfect example. Dirty clothes and laundry soap are necessary functional items but they end up scattered all over the place. Instant visual mayhem! Fortunately, the solutions are often easy and inexpensive.

While working with Susan, a single mother of two, I noted that visual clutter was a source of stress. Cleaning supplies, toys, and coats for all types of weather were piled everywhere. Although all the items were appropriate and necessary for her household, the visual clutter grated on her nerves. She didn't have a lot of time or a big budget to dedicate to solutions and she was stymied.

As a first step, we gathered the cleaning supplies in an inexpensive storage container. This hid the chaos while keeping the supplies easily accessible. We then moved the coat rack behind the door. In the family room, a handful of wicker baskets that tucked into the shelves like drawers created storage for all the kids' toys. As an added bonus, they made it easier for the children to clean up after themselves!

Although visual clutter can be objects, it often shows up as piles of paper. A few pieces waiting to be looked at attract a handful of unopened mail. Receipts, insurance forms and school permission slips migrate to the pile. Soon the cluster becomes a magnet for brochures, fliers and unread magazines. The clutter magnet then attracts broken gadgets, wounded dolls, and bags full of recently bought items waiting to be put away. It fills the environment with nagging reminders of everything that still needs to be done.

**Find Your Home's Visual Chaos**

Since we're all at different points in our lives, we all have different kinds of items we consider necessary. Lego bricks, medications, college catalogues, diapering supplies and job applications might be some of yours. What is your life stage, and what necessities are connected to that stage?

The papers that started the chain reaction are likely important, or at least they were important at some point in time. They've just ended up in the wrong place. Once you've set up your Flourishing Home hubs, you won't have this problem anymore. You'll open mail standing next to your bill paying hub. School permission slips will be pinned to the command central board. After the slips are signed, they'll be shifted to the children's homework area so they can be returned the next day.

Sounds dreamy, right? Well, it's more than just a fantasy. It's your Flourishing Home at work!

### 3. Invisible Clutter

It's time to put on your detective hat. We're going to look beyond the obvious for another kind of clutter hidden in every home. On the surface, a house can appear neat and well organized. But open any closet or drawer and things spill out. *Junk drawer* is a term I bet we can all relate to. Many people go one step further and create a junk closet. I've even been in homes that have junk *rooms!*

It's all invisible clutter. This type of clutter is more common than you might think. Earlier I mentioned my client Jane. Her home's overall foundation supported her wellness and wellbeing. It reflected the feelings she wished to evoke along with her and her family's values. Positive primes like pictures of loved ones, a watercolor of a beloved dog, and furniture bought during memorable trips dotted her environment.

She'd even set up a hub as the family's command center. The children had their own hobby hubs. But the surface was deceiving. She was experiencing a great deal of frustration trying to maintain schedules, notices, appointments and other obligations. Often these were written on paper, so her hubs were covered with sticky notes, copies of emails, calendars and fliers. She desperately wanted less stuff and more organization.

---

### Idea Spark: Eliminate Avoidance

Set a timer for a very short time, say three or five minutes. Tackle one area of clutter. This tactic works because anyone can do something for a few minutes. When the bell dings, you'll be surprised by how much you've accomplished.

---

Clearly we had to start at her command central. With her approval… her *hesitant* approval…I opened a cabinet. Papers immediately tumbled out. We both jumped to catch them before they ended up in a heap on the floor. "That's just like me," she said. "I'm put together on the outside but messy on the inside!"

Can anyone else out there relate to that? She had a beautiful home but was stressed out because too much stuff had been stuffed into her cabinets! That, dear reader, is the definition of invisible clutter.

Usually the Home Wellness Detective walkthrough is performed start to finish without any advice from me no matter what I spot along the way. By leaving all the comments until later, clients can share their deepest clutter secrets and their most frustrating organization issues without feeling judged. For Jane, I decided to offer an intervention on the spot. It was a risk, but in her case I knew it would pay off immediately.

We set a timer for five minutes and went at it. Out went the Christmas cards that had no function other than to make her feel guilty whenever she thought about getting rid of them. Out went four extra phonebooks that had been tossed mindlessly into the cabinets. User manuals for a variety of products she no longer owned were recycled. By the time the bell went off, we'd filled two trash bags! Using a few simple strategies, we'd monumentally increased the efficiency of her informational hub.

---

### Idea Spark: Maximize Usage

Do you have an unused or underutilized area of your home that could become a functional hub? Diane repurposed her unused formal dining room to create a homework hub. My family redefined our formal living room, a space we used a handful of times in twelve years, into a functional hub we use every day!

---

It's amazing how much can be accomplished in a short period of time. After Jane tackled the invisible clutter in the command center, she realized that organizing really wasn't overwhelming. We set the timer for ten minutes and tackled her children's school project closet (the hobby hub). We filled two more trash bags with dried-out markers, half-used stickers pages from long-ago preschool days, torn construction paper, and scraps that were too small to save for other projects.

As an added bonus, we found unopened school supplies. She didn't have to spend more money to buy duplicates, and she didn't have to waste time shopping for those items. Considering that magical combination, decluttering just might turn you into a Flourishing Home genie!

If you'll forgive me for talking about another children's show, read on! Barney had a clean-up song. It was short and sweet, and kids cleaned a small area while singing along. Find your own special song and let music help you tackle one clutter area every week.

You are hereby officially granted permission to disregard the traditional use of different rooms and areas. I'll be your personal cheerleader as you charge into using each space in a way that fits you best. Think outside the box and get your Flourishing Home to work for you!

**Takeaway:** Functional, hobby and information hubs are the action centers of your home. A command central is key to the efficient, smooth operation of your family's castle. Set up hubs in your household and you'll reap the benefits of a Flourishing Home today!

# CHAPTER FIVE

# HEARTS

*Q*uick: What's the one thing that could happen to make you happy? Bagging that big promotion? Winning the lottery? Maybe you'd opt for a new car. No matter which one you pick, you'd be wrong. A social survey that has been conducted since the early 1970s polled over 53,000 people on this question. What made them happiest wasn't wealth or work. It was their family relationships.

Creating a flourishing heart where your family and friends can be nurtured is truly important. The heart of a Flourishing Home is any place where people gather. The occasion might be informal or formal, and the space to which they gravitate might be soothing or invigorating. The flourishing heart strengthens relationships by providing a place where conversations and interactions bloom. It provides everyone with safety, comfort, and authenticity.

## Find Your Heart

The kitchen's function, and the need for it within the home often make it the place where people spend time with friends and family. Since it's so important, the kitchen is discussed in length later in the chapter, but before we do that, consider the rest of your Flourishing Home. Strip away how the space functions and whether the space is necessary. Focus purely on the spots where you enjoy spending time with people. Which areas do you think of? Which rooms do you gravitate to when function or personal refueling isn't the goal? Does your home have "pure hearts?"

Often hearts are found in conventional spaces like the family room. As always, we're going to free ourselves of the old ways of thinking! Consider the unconventional areas where people might gather. A swing set can be the heart of a new family. The driveway where you and your teenager shoot hoops becomes a heart for a maturing family. The front stoop or townhouse balcony that hosts an impromptu glass of wine with a neighbor becomes a heart for friendship. A basement done up as a playroom becomes an authentic, safe place for children. These are pure hearts— spaces that nurture your family, support your friends, and create bonds among every member of your family.

A home's pure hearts can change over time. As the young child grows and graduates to shooting hoops outside, the family heart shifts from the basement to the driveway. No matter where you and your family are in their development, the home's hearts will be products of everyone who lives there. Becoming mindful of these hearts and how they function helps you foster positive relationships and positive emotions. Those elements in turn fuel the spirit. Every heart therefore impacts all the different elements of wellness and wellbeing.

How is a heart different from a hub, a transition point, or a space dedicated to refueling? A hub's defining characteristics are task-oriented. Transition points focus on movement into and out of certain spaces, routines or roles. Spiritual refueling areas are extremely personal, often private, and touch upon those innermost desires we share only with our higher power. Hearts, quite simply, are places of gathering.

Just as wellness and wellbeing influence each other, a heart also claims its own identity but can overlap with other areas of the home. By looking at the characteristics of other areas of the home, the definition of a home heart becomes clear. For example, Dave was a small business owner. His wife Cyndi worked part-time outside the home and full time in the home as a mother of three. Particularly with a newborn on hand, their lives were moving wildly. The moments spent sharing a laugh or eye-to-eye in conversation were few and far between.

Monitoring homework assignments while folding laundry and organizing the bills left them feeling disconnected. Their interactions with the children were becoming more functional. It seemed like all they ever said were things like, "Did you do your homework?" "Please put away your toys." "Can someone entertain the baby?" They both recognized the need to connect with each other and with their children in a less task-oriented way.

While I worked with the family, they mentioned how much they enjoyed the swing set. There they came together for conversation, playtime, and family fun. This was a true heart for their growing family.

While the backyard swing set can be a family's heart, it might not work that way for a couple. Life often pulls us in many directions. Work and family obligations can overwhelm even the most organized and devoted couples. Do you have a place within your home that qualifies as a heart for you and your significant other? Certain phases of life can make authentic, comfortable, safe conversations challenging. The current life phase my husband and I are in challenges us to connect. In six years our children will be out on their own and quiet moments, ripe for meaningful conversation, will arise without effort. Now, however, we are in the midst of the college application procedure, standardized test preparation, dance and soccer schedules, and the general obligations of work and home. An evening spent on the back porch snuggling for a few minutes before lights out helps us stay connected.

Creating a couple's heart inside the Flourishing Home can help two people connect. Special relationships can be enjoyed more deeply by creating spaces or becoming mindful of places that help each person connect with the others. The trickle down effect of positive relationships, especially between significant others living under the same roof, can generate a flood of positive effects on happiness and health. Think about the spaces in your home that could be a heart for you and your special someone.

## Merging Spaces

If you look around your home and just can't find a perfect gathering place, consider repurposing rooms or areas to create new hearts. If the heart overlaps with other purposes, don't worry! Every space in your home can be used in more than one way. This was the case with Corrie. One of her favorite areas was a repurposed living room where she and her children gathered. The kids did their homework, she managed the household, and afterward everyone cuddled on the couch to read. Suzan's formal living room was where she meditated and where she welcomed visitors during yoga mini-retreats. This one area functioned as both a heart and a spiritual refueling space.

If the only time you can really catch up with a loved one is while they're walking on a treadmill, then by all means move a comfy chair into the exercise room. Add a trio of stools to the center island in the kitchen so one spouse can pay bills and chat while the other cooks dinner. And who's to say a yoga area can't fit inside a library? Anything that allows you to gather together, even if individuals are performing separate activities, creates a Flourishing Home heart. If it truly reflects the interests of those living under your roof, it will serve the wellbeing of your entire family.

While working with clients and looking at how they use their homes, we often talk about repurposing rooms to accommodate activities that truly reflect their desires. Sometimes a traditional formal area can become a hobby or functional hub. I've also encountered individuals and families who gather in certain areas, including their dining rooms, but who don't enjoy the spaces.

That was the case with Celeste. Her kitchen was clearly a functional hub for meal preparation, but it wasn't a heart. The family valued time spent together and wanted to share meals but didn't have a space that pulled them together. Their dining room decorations consisted of hand-me-down furniture that carried negative emotional baggage. The 1970's country oak dining set contrasted too much with the minimalist white lines of the rest of the living space.

Through our discussion, Celeste became mindful of her underlying feelings. She addressed them with a few actions that weren't overwhelming in terms of time or money. With the support of the immediate family, she got rid of the china cabinet. By eliminating the largest piece of furniture, she immediately changed immediately the room's energy. The dining chairs were repurposed as game table chairs in the basement. A white linen floor-length tablecloth masked the remaining piece of furniture. The room felt more in line with the family's style. Because of that change it became a heart, a place of comfort where friends and family could share meals. Her positive relationships grew!

As you search your Flourishing Home for heart centers, think about how people really live in your home. If your formal dining room is used only twice a year during holidays, it's not serving your household well. You still have to clean the space, you're still paying rent or mortgage for that space, and your family might be cramped inside smaller rooms that are used every day. Never hesitate to unleash that blue sky thinking and repurpose rooms that just aren't working. Otherwise you might find that they become obstacles to building your Flourishing Home.

## Building Blocks for the Heart

When creating a home heart, consider a few basic elements. In personal areas like the master bedroom, you'll be able to focus only on the needs of the people who gather there. Public areas where you entertain will consider the visitors you invite into your home. In every case, think about the elements described here to optimize everyone's wellbeing.

**Seating.** Is there a comfy spot for everyone who usually gathers there? Do you have a way to expand seating as needed? Benches that double as storage containers are a great option. In a pinch, an ottoman can also become a place to sit.

**Lighting.** Does the available light support the area's activities without being overwhelming? Open drapes to let sunshine pour in. In the summer, consider opaque fabric blinds that allow light to filter through while trapping heat against the glass. What type of lighting is best for evening hours? Overhead lights can be used as they were originally installed or you can attach a dimmer switch. Pay attention to the special needs of different tasks and add table lamps or clip-on lights to those areas.

**Layout.** Does the position of the furniture foster interaction? Seating should be close enough together to encourage conversation. If not, consider using your temporary seating options like ottomans and storage chests to foster intimacy.

**Congruency.** Is the area in line with the needs and desires of the people who use the space? Young children need plenty of room to move around. Older children might want desktops or lap desks for their hobbies or homework. Adults might like throw pillows for extra support.

Using these guidelines, let's revisit Dave and Cyndi. The swing set was a comfy spot for the kids to play. The parents enjoyed face-to-face interaction with their children and each other. There was plenty of space that allowed other kids and caregivers to join the fun. The light and outdoor ambience fed their need to be in a natural setting. The heart was in line with the value they placed on family bonds: parent to parent, parent to child, and sibling to sibling. They even included their "adopted" family of neighbors and friends!

Some hearts might not have every one of the items we've mentioned in this section while others will have all of them and more. How you build each heart space will depend on the needs, goals and desires of your entire family.

## The Kitchen as the Heart

In the Flourishing Home, the kitchen directly impacts many elements of wellness and wellbeing. Proper nutrition and eating behaviors affect the physical elements of wellness. By also fostering positive relationships and emotions, the kitchen positively impacts happiness and wellbeing. Because this area plays such a powerful role in our daily lives, much of this chapter is dedicated to creating a heart within this functional hub.

By far one of the most important things you can do to foster wellness and wellbeing is to cook and eat meals in your Flourishing

**Heart of the Home**

When asked to locate the heart of your home, it's pretty likely you'll say the kitchen. Most of us spend a good amount of time there; the kitchen is a functional hub. Since so many areas in a typical home serve more than one function, it's no surprise that the kitchen is also a place where family and friends gather.

Home. It makes sense…you have control over which foods are provided as well as portion size. But that tends to be easier said than done. Over the past several decades, the average time Americans spend together as a family during mealtime has dropped 33 percent. During that same period, fast food sales grew from a $6 billion a year business in 1970 to over $184 billion in 2010. This is in part due to the difficulty of shopping for groceries, preparing the food, cooking, and cleaning up afterward.

Keep reading! Trust me, I'm one of those people who hate repetitive tasks. Things like laundry, cleaning, grocery shopping and yes, cooking are at the top of my "pulling teeth" list. No matter how painful these tasks might be on certain days, they still get done. My Flourishing Home supports this fundamental element. My family reaps the rewards in terms of physical health and the quality time we spend together.

You only have to modify one or two elements to increase the amount of cooking and eating you do in your Flourishing Home. The benefits will always outshine the effort. Although there aren't many guarantees in life, this is one guarantee I can offer without any doubts! A whole host of positive results are possible. This section highlights some of the best.

**Better nutrition.** When we eat at home, the nutrition we receive is generally of a higher quality. Children who share dinner with a family eat fewer fatty foods and receive higher amounts of fiber, minerals and vitamins. People of all ages tend to opt for less-healthy food when they eat out. The roll made from bleached white flour instead of a whole-grain option from the pantry, the milkshake instead of water, the cheeseburger instead of salad... all those selections are so easy to make when faced with a menu loaded with choices.

Remember what I said earlier about willpower being a muscle. Fewer choices means you'll be less fatigued. When you're more alert, you'll make better choices. Ah, what a lovely circular cycle! It all leads back to eating at home.

**Healthy Tools**

Do you have the tools on hand that will make cooking at home easy and healthy? Consider whether your household will benefit from a steamer, a clay cooking pot, a slow cooker, an oil mister, a blender or a juicer. The investment you'll make in the purchase will pay off at the first meal.

**Decreased obesity.** Forgive me, five-star chefs, for what I'm about to say: Restaurants want repeat business. Food offered by any café, restaurant or grill is made to taste good. Too often that means loading up the extras like butter, cream, salt, fat and sugar. Few offerings are focused on your physical health. So those French fries are high fat, salty starch dipped in ketchup, which is itself loaded with sugar and salt. It's not healthy yet it keeps us coming back for more!

Oh, and let's not forget portion sizes! One study showed that restaurants were offering portions two to four times larger than a regular meal. In terms of wellness and wellbeing, more is definitely less valuable!

## The Dinner Hour

When dinnertime rolls around are you too busy, too tired, too overloaded by technology or too tempted by the ease of fast food to sit and enjoy a meal? The obstacles are real and can feel rather weighty. If you list the obstacles side by side with the benefits of making that effort, the pendulum swings right over to the benefits.

For families, a shared dinner hour decreases depression and eating disorders like bulimia and anorexia. Children who share family meals are less likely to become overweight or consider suicide. At home meals kids eat more veggies, learn manners, pick up a wider vocabulary, and end up performing better in school. Children feel loved and teenagers may even delay their first sexual encounter longer.

Some statistics say that the average family dines together at home four times per week. Ten percent of families only eat together twice a week. Take a minute to reflect on what happens under your roof. Our family places a high value on family dinners, so much so that my husband and I compare calendars to make sure we can eat together. Even so, we struggle to reach four every week. We fall somewhere between the average of four and the low of two.

As the parents of three children, each of whom has different passions ranging from dance and music to sports alongside academic and work schedules, the family dinner is often elusive. When our schedules allow, the family gathering is mandatory. While we often hear a groan from our teenager, at some point our conversation falls "in the zone." Our discussion isn't forced or directed by any agenda. We enter into a relationship with our children. Their activities change and their independence grows all the time but the benefits of eating together help them in ways we can't even measure.

**Research**

One study that spanned twenty-five years and thousand of families discovered some of the keys to thriving families. Their households demonstrated commitment to each other, appreciation and affection between members, fostered positive communication, spent time together, valued their spiritual wellbeing, and focused on the ability to cope with stress. All six of those traits can be garnered by taking one proactive step: family dinners. Wow! That's quite a list of benefits!

## Dining Solo

Whether you're the sole resident, are part of a traditional family or live in a blended mix, honor the dinner hour. The benefits of mindfully sharing a meal are innumerable. Mindless eating, on the other hand, is a negative behavior that unfortunately is extremely easy to fall into.

Dinner for a single person, for example, can often take the path of least resistance. Quick bites of something heated in the microwave then eaten in front of the television is a too-familiar scene for many single clients I've worked with. Even people who live with others fall into the trap of mindlessly taking meals while multitasking. Grabbing a plate of food and scattering in different directions to check email, start homework or catch up on the news devalues the act of nourishment.

---

### Idea Spark: Alternatives to Mealtime

If your family just can't eat dinner as a group, see if everyone can make it to breakfast. A post-dinner gathering around a cup of coffee, tea or a light dessert might also fill the bill. Brunch can often be squeezed into weekends packed with sports and hobby activities. Whenever mealtimes approach, make them special!

---

I love working with different people and have had the opportunity to counsel some amazing single women. One relatively common hurdle to mindful eating is dinner at the end of a long workday. Rachel talked about finding comfort in eating in front of the television. The food prep was often minimal, often reheated in the microwave and sometimes eaten straight out of the container. The act of nourishing her body was done without much thought to taste, enjoyment, or the signals of satiety.

While brainstorming about a simple shift in habits, she committed to preparing an eye-pleasing tray she could carry into the living room. The television was entertainment and helped her transition from work to home, so it wasn't eliminated. But the act of nourishing her body was honored by the preparation of a beautiful dinner setting including silverware, appropriately sized dishes, stemware, and a lit candle. The extra couple of minutes spent honoring the dinner meal translated into mindful eating.

She enjoyed the food more, ate more appropriate servings, transitioned into a more relaxed mindset, and was able to hear her body's signal that she was full.

Whether you're alone or with others, the opportunity to enjoy the flavors and sensations of the food should take center stage. Singles and every member of a busy household should bring awareness, pleasure and value to mealtimes. Mindful eating, eating only when you're truly hungry, and enjoying the food that goes into your body are all important. Know what you're eating, how much you're eating, and where you have the meal. When you're full, stop eating. How can you pay attention to that moment if you're too busy with other matters?

> **Plate It!**
>
> When eating at home, bring food to the table on plates. Restaurants plate your food because they're bringing the entire portion. Often at home we serve family style with heaping bowls in the middle of the table. This encourages mindless eating. With the exception of vegetables, plate everything before placing it in front of your family.

Shared meals can refuel the spirit as well as the body. By drawing attention to the time you're spending together and marking the moment as important, you bring mindfulness to the act. This is an ideal time to express gratitude. This single feeling is *uber* important to happiness and wellbeing!

Prayers are a common way to begin a meal with an expression of gratitude. They can be traditional or spur of the moment; they can follow a specific denomination or simply offer thanks. Think outside the box here, too! Encourage your family to create their own traditions. Our family keeps small notebooks by the dinner table. Each of us writes down three things we're grateful for and why we believe the events occurred. The notes can be shared or they can stay private.

## Idea Spark: Single Love

If you're single or work at home and eat a lot of meals on your own, set a beautiful table. Take the time to enjoy every bite. Treat yourself as a guest! Make eating a physical act of refueling as well as a moment to refuel your spirit. Treat yourself well. Treat yourself with love!

Your family can find something special too. Light a candle to remind everyone of the shining light that is your God. Turn off electronic devices so that every person can be fully tuned to the others sitting at the table. Create the best mood possible, then repeat those same actions at every meal. And be patient, consistent, and determined. We still hear groans when the mini-journals come out, yet every one of us reaches for our pens. The tradition is so ingrained we really can't do without it!

---

### Idea Spark: Helping Hands

More and more grocery stores offer shopping services. For a nominal cost, say $10, someone will shop for your groceries, scan them at the checkout counter, bag them and put them in your car when you pull up. How long does it take you to do that yourself? Let's say the average grocery run takes two hours. Is your time worth more than $5 per hour?

---

Congratulations! You've just added two hours to your schedule. You can devote that time to increasing your happiness, health, and rock the world attitude. If it makes you feel better, it's priceless. If someone out there offers a service that can help you recapture more time, weigh the payout against the payoff. It might be worth it!

## Back Pocket Meals

One of the biggest obstacles to having your kitchen serve as a pure heart is lack of time. To help you take a giant step forward, I'm going to introduce you to one of my family's best Flourishing Home tips: Back pocket meals.

Back pocket meals are simple entrees that are easy to prepare. They combat the too busy, too tired, or too stressed excuses that keep families from eating together. In addition to being easy, everyone under your roof should like them. If you dedicate a little time to creating a list that works for your Flourishing Home, then putting together a meal during a busy time won't seem so overwhelming. Here are a few things that work in our house. And since they come from a person who hates to cook yet who values healthy, yummy, easy food everyone will eat, they'll make great stepping stones for your own list!

*Break out the wok.* Choose your favorite protein, trim the fat if necessary, and sauté in a healthy oil like olive or grape seed. Add vegetables with different colors and textures, then serve. We even sneak whole grain rice into this meal to round out the portions.

*Rumertoff.* I love this one! Clay cooking at its best is easy, delicious, and doesn't involve too much cleanup. Basically you toss a bunch of stuff into a clay pot and slow cook it. Our favorite is chicken with vegetables—carrots, potatoes, onions and celery along with a healthy dose of garlic. One pot means cleanup is always a breeze. We usually have leftovers that make a great chicken salad the next day. Sometimes we use the leftovers as the base for a veggie-enhanced soup that can be frozen until the next time we have a crazy evening.

*Chili.* Take a whole bunch of beans, then add veggies and some protein. Our favorites include a white bean chicken chili and traditional chili made with ground turkey. The great thing is that you can freeze it or store it in single portion sizes. You can also freeze a big batch and whip it out for your next group meal.

*Slow cooker.* Over the next two months, try a new recipe every week that looks like it might work for your family. Hopefully you'll walk away with two or three that are healthy, easy, and a big hit.

*Placement of dish ware.* Sometimes the simple, easy tweaks can pay huge dividends. Deborah spent the majority of her discovery session and walkthrough talking about functional activity hubs. During the final thirty minutes, we breezed through the placement of different items in the kitchen heart. I suggested she move the larger plates to a higher shelf and put the smaller, more appropriate serving plates on the most accessible shelf. She took action right away. The smaller plates improved her family's eating behaviors and generated a beneficial change in weight for both parents.

## It's All in the Heart

Some of these tools, tactics, and tricks will resonate with you more than others. The matrix of available time crossed by finances crossed with the need for intervention crossed with desire…wow, again there's a multitude of possible solutions! Breathe. Will thirty minutes spent preparing single serving sizes once a week pay off with healthy nutrition and eating behaviors? Then schedule thirty minutes of prep time. Make it a priority. Do you have the financial resource to get some help? If paying a bit more for a tray of sliced fruits and vegetables is key to consuming more fresh food then prioritize your budget.

You might find that one simple tool, maybe a measuring implement, has a trickle down effect that creates monumental benefits. Whatever resonates with you, whatever positive change or small or large adjustments you make will be personal. There are a lot of great ideas in this chapter, so start with one or two. Be consistent, determined and patient. Put aside perfection and strive to use them most of the time. The little things will add up without making you feel overwhelmed.

**Takeaway:** The hearts of your Flourishing Home serve you, your family, friends and guests.

CHAPTER SIX

# REFUELING

"*Ahh*, I needed that."

Do you ever have that response to an activity, person, outing or experience? I don't mean the chocolate that curbs a craving, but the experience that fills your soul. The sun on your back as you wade through cool waves... the sermon that reignites compassion ... finishing a great book while sitting in a comfy chair by the fire... the musical performance that moves you to tears... a great night's sleep in the coziest of beds.

What inspires you? What moves you emotionally? What reignites your passion and fills your spiritual tank? Even if nothing leaps to your mind right now, by the end of this chapter you'll have more insight into the answers. You'll find places within your home that refill, refuel and revitalize you on a deeply personal level. By integrating these elements into your Flourishing Home, you'll respect your spirit by nurturing, supporting and soothing your soul.

## The Core of Wellness

In the previous chapters, we've done a lot already to get your house, apartment or condo to work for you. Ultimately, though, your home is your sanctuary. You want its primes to be positive, the transition points and hubs to work smoothly, the hearts to be welcoming, and the environment to be happy and healthy. Even if every one of these aspects of a Flourishing Home operates with precision, the people who live there can still be running on empty spiritually.

It's too easy to shuffle spiritual refueling to the bottom of the list while keeping up with our daily lives. Research had proven that proper eating behaviors, nutrition, exercise, activity levels, health and stress management are all beneficial. The spiritual elements of wellness are a bit trickier. The questions arise largely because the soul element of the mind/body/spirit connection is an intensely personal concept.

The Dalai Lama explains that spirituality can be discussed in terms of the specific religious beliefs people hold or in terms of kindness, compassion and caring at the core of each. The core elements are far more important. Everyone needs to focus on those elements no matter what kinds of religious traditions they might follow. Really it's all about love…loving and being loved. When you exercise love, you find true peace. More happiness, less stress, and a little peace now and then…sign me up!

The definition of spirituality and the solutions that serve you best lie within you and your home. My task in this chapter is first to help you locate the feelings that support your spirituality. Then I'll help you translate those feelings into elements inside your Flourishing Home. We'll start with the most straightforward areas and work our way down to the smallest spots. Every bit of it will fill your spiritual tank!

### Personal Space

"That's it! I'm putting myself in time-out."

I've uttered this phrase more than once as I marched myself upstairs to the master bedroom. Usually it happens when I need a break or have reached a breaking point. No matter why I declare one, a time-out gives me a little space and time to retreat, to be free of chores and obligations. After a few minutes or a few hours, I'm ready to face life with a refreshed mind and a refueled attitude.

To support these mini retreats, my time-out space is luxurious. The couch is loaded with soft blankets and cushy pillows. The seating is positioned so that I have a beautiful view through the window, and an aromatic candle stands nearby. The space is a tiny oasis in the private area of my home. It belongs solely to me, and allows much-needed self-care to be accessible any time of day or night.

A personal space can be anything from a comfy chair to a dedicated meditation space. Whether you claim a small corner or an entire room as your time-out area, the space has unlimited spiritual refueling capabilities.

Usually these sanctuaries are located in a private area of the home where you can be free to safely express yourself. Once there, you can recite your calming chants, pray, repeat personal affirmations or meditate. You might also read, listen to music, or enjoy a moment of silence.

Spirituality requires patience, compassion, emotional control and maturity… all things that grow weaker as we are worn down by ambient noise, workday stresses, an overwhelming list of chores, and other daily events. Remember when we discussed good stress? Even that can wear you down! To be at your spiritual best, you need to relieve your burdens, manage stress, focus on creating true happiness, feel a genuine sense of calm, and seek peace. The Flourishing Home offers a place dedicated to your spiritual refueling.

These spaces can arise in the most unlikely spots. Corrine, a DIY guru and mother of two, struggled with a master bath makeover. The room was rather spacious and felt awkward to her. She tried several pieces of small furniture to make the room more cozy without success. During our brainstorming session, the idea of installing a dressing table and small chair arose.

**Ahh, I Needed That!**

- What aspect of your wellness or wellbeing needs a boost?
- What activities, experiences, people, sounds, sights or smells trigger the *I needed that!* response?
- Which object in your Flourishing Home represents that feeling, activity, experience or person?

Although a dressing table usually supports intensely physical care—the application and removal of makeup, a place to apply lotion before retiring for the evening, a storage and display area for perfume—she knew it could become something more. After all, she would use the area twice a day every day of the year. She began by selecting a chair that offered as much comfort as support. Then she added candles and music.

Every time she sat at the table, she symbolically refueled her spiritual tank. A spot that might have totaled all of four square feet served her wellness and her wellbeing. And that truly is the best the Flourishing Home has to offer. By giving herself the best possible experience in the concrete, physical aspects of self-care, she created the best possible experience in self-care for her soul.

## Your Own Private Paradise

Ultimately, how you create your personal space and what it will offer will be highly personal. Since this spot is vital to your overall wellness and wellbeing, take this opportunity to consider only your own needs. Give yourself total freedom and gear up that blue sky creativity. There really are no rules!

First choose a spot in your home that feels right to you. Some people want to tuck into a corner while others enjoy a feeling of open space. Think about the views the spot commands. A loft that overlooks your living room gives you a bird's-eye view while a window looking onto the yard will be lush and green. Bring in the sense of smell by adding a scented candle, air freshener, or a vase of flowers cut from your garden.

Pay close attention to the sounds you'll likely hear while using your retreat. Setting up your time-out space along the wall that is shared with your teenaged son might expose you to some music you don't enjoy! Other sounds to be conscious of are kitchen cabinets or pots banging, toilets flushing, and the hammering of fingers on a keyboard. Remember too that outside sounds can creep in. Birds twittering next to a feeder will set a very different tone than wood being ripped by power tools in the shed.

Finally, consider the textures. A chair upholstered in corduroy is going to be a very different experience than one done up in crushed velvet. Having a sweat jacket nearby to throw on will be different than snuggling under a velour blanket. A glass side table will look and feel different than one with a wood or marble top. Everything from the carpet to the ceiling can be textured, so let your ideas expand!

Next, clean the space thoroughly. As you work, be aware of the kind of lighting, furniture, art and accessories you would like in that space. Always return to how you'll use the area. A reading center will need different accessories than a music listening station. A spot to enjoy total solitude will need visual screens while a meditation area might require that exterior sounds be dampened. Only those items that will help you experience a calm and peaceful time should be present.

When you've considered all these elements together, you've created a spiritual refueling center. My client Kim was drawn to the sunlit, airy room that traditionally would be considered a living room. During the Foundation Discovery part of the Wellness Walkthrough, she clearly voiced many of her values, interests and goals. Her primary frustration came from...you guessed it, the living room. Although she liked the space, she had no idea how to utilize it. By setting up a personal foundation, she envisioned, then created, an area that supported her yoga practice

The room became her personal refueling area. After the negative primes in the environment were removed and downsized, she cleared the frustrating energy that had driven her away before. In its place, the shelving was accessorized with positive primes like the dried flowers from her son's wedding. The desk she'd disliked became a yogi-like altar with candles and a collection of yoga figurines. She transformed the room into a place that offered her a deeply nurturing experience.

**Building Your Personal Space**

- Is the space free of distractions?
- Do you have what you need at hand to maximize refueling?
- What one change would make this the best possible personal space for you?

## Sleeping in Paradise

For some people, the bedroom is a place to sleep and also a personal space. Children, teens and adults often utilize their bedrooms for its basic features (sleeping, changing clothes, and physical care) and as a place to enjoy a little privacy. For many people, the bedroom often takes on even more roles. This single space becomes both a retreat and a place to nurture the spirit. For children and teens in particular, the room is a place in which people can be social, a place where they can explore new thoughts and ideas, and a place that reflects their identity. It can also hold a personal activity hub or a hobby hub.

Because these areas can be used for so many purposes, ensuring that they're efficient spiritual refueling centers can be challenging. Because secondary bedrooms tend to be much smaller than other rooms, sometimes significantly so, the challenges multiply. Creativity is your best partner for reshaping these spaces.

The family who'd lost their mother to cancer had two daughters. While the younger girl wanted a quirky, funky room that reflected her identity, sixteen-year-old Kacee needed a room that was much different than her sister's. First and foremost, she needed a retreat in which to heal. The ability to express herself through art was critical to who she was and how she felt about her life. She also wanted to be able to open her windows but a set of broken blinds blocked her access.

Her mini-makeover began with a thorough cleaning, decluttering and reorganization. Once we knew exactly what kinds of physical objects we had at hand, we thoughtfully arranged the room to meet her spiritual needs. A private art studio with all her supplies was set up. The broken blinds were replaced with fabric panels that created total darkness to enhance her sleep. By day, they were easily pulled up. The view was peaceful and the sun streaming in illuminated her art and refueled her spirit.

The key points for setting up a secondary bedroom are things we've already discussed: Declutter to promote peace. Use positive primes that trigger your inner yogi. Create hubs that are efficient and bring in those blue-sky thoughts. Serve your spiritual wellbeing first and the rest will follow!

## The Flourishing Grail

What if your Flourishing Home could hand you the Holy Grail of wellness and wellbeing? Drinking from this particular cup will help you shed extra pounds and maintain a healthy weight; help you adhere to your exercise regiment; help you be more productive, have more patience, enjoy a better memory and strengthen your ability to concentrate. You'll be less irritable, less anxious and less depressed. Sip daily from this cup to decrease your risk for a host of medical conditions including hypertension, diabetes, heart disease, periodontal issues and metabolic disorders.

This grail isn't as elusive as you might think. It's certainly not as elusive as all the buzz about diet and exercise. A healthy lifestyle consists of eating the right food in the right quantity and getting enough exercise, yet 35% of Americans are obese. Another 30% are overweight. For a whopping 65% of us, diet and exercise clearly aren't working!

I have great news! I'm going to tell you about the one thing that's as important…maybe even more important…than good nutrition and eating behaviors. You only have to make one adjustment to your life to reap all the rewards. In today's world, it's a solution that's frequently overlooked;

fortunately, the Flourishing Home has the answer. To truly improve your wellness and wellbeing, and to enjoy those improvements for the rest of your life, you need one simple thing: sleep.

## A Sleepy Nation

Your bedroom or sleeping environment is critical, vital, the pinnacle of importance for spiritual refueling, wellness and wellbeing. Yet according to the National Sleep Foundation, 50% of Americans are sleep deprived. Over half report daytime sleepiness, and 37% are so sleepy it interferes with daily activities (like, um, exercise?!). For women between the ages of thirty and sixty, 16% sleep less than six hours per night.

Drowsiness and inattention are one thing. The lesser-known fallout from too little sleep shows up in our bodies. Recently scientists discovered the hormones gherlin and leptin, which send messages to the brain to either eat more or to stop eating. Sleep-deprived people have an 18% decrease in leptin and a 28% increase in gherlin. That boosts their appetites 24 percent! If you're a woman, the burden is even greater because our bodies have to work very hard to keep those levels balanced. When these regulators are out of commission, your hunger signals blast right through that red light as if it wasn't even there!

Lack of sleep also throws our minds and emotions out of whack. When your body needs rest, it craves comfort. If you don't get enough sleep, the body seeks that comfort from food. And what's the fastest path to comfort from food? Fat, sugar, and simple carbs like bread and pasta. It's a diet disaster waiting to happen! Getting by on four or five hours of sleep makes that doughnut look more tempting while a fast-food burger seems irresistible!

Unless you have a medical issue or are in those first months after pregnancy, one of the biggest things standing between you and too many pounds is willpower. But willpower is very much like a muscle...it grows tired. That's why most of us can make all kinds of great decisions in the morning only to splurge on a chocolate chip cookie late that afternoon. How many times have you scheduled a workout for the end of the day only to trade your sneakers for slippers? Your willpower has been drained by the judgments, decisions and activities of everyday life.

One proven way to restore and replenish your willpower muscle is sleep. Every time you go to bed late, you're actually dealing yourself a double whammy. In addition to the hunger hormones, there's human growth hormone. HGH controls the proportion of fat to muscle. HGH also strongly supports our immune systems, so sleep deprivation makes us more susceptible to infection and illness.

Prolonged stress and sleep deprivation also increase cortisol, the hormone that triggers our fight-or-flight response. This survival mechanism encourages our bodies to store energy in the form of fat, especially around the midsection. A single night of poor sleep affects the way we process sugar. Our bodies will function like someone who has diabetes or pre-diabetes. Insulin resistance starts a domino effect for all kinds of medical issues.

Although we often notice those nights when we only grab a few hours of sleep, losing just a half hour of rest over a prolonged period can create the same results. If you feel tired in the afternoon, can't get by without a nap, or need to catch up on sleep during weekends, you're suffering from a lack of sleep. Falling asleep right away, falling asleep while reading or watching TV, relying on an alarm clock, and hitting the snooze button repeatedly are also signs. If you're well rested you should wake up around the same time every morning, even on weekends, before your alarm goes off.

Sleep deprivation can be caused by stress, caffeine, alcohol, smoking, irregular hours, age, jet lag, kids, pets, technological devices, violent TV shows, disturbing news reports, an uncomfortable environment, and uncomfortable bedding. If you're the first person to raise a hand and shout," Me, me, me!" when asked, "Who would like to get enough sleep every night?" then read on. The Flourishing Home can make that happen.

## The Magic Number

In my work, I've helped a variety of women, from single mothers to corporate executives. All wanted to improve their wellness and wellbeing through weight loss, stress management, or better physical fitness. While discussing their sleep habits, I discovered that over half of them didn't get enough rest! If you think you're genetically wired for less than eight hours of sleep, you're part of only 3% of the population. Either you're very lucky or you're fooling yourself!

While individual needs do have a genetic component, a lack of sleep will catch up with everyone. Adults need five rapid-eye movement (REM) cycles -the time during which we dream—to restore, replenish and renew their bodies and minds. Four states during which you don't dream precede each REM period, and the entire set takes between 90 to 120 minutes. To get five full stages, you have to sleep seven to ten hours per night.

**Bedtime Brainstorm**

Take a few minutes to think about your bedtime ritual. Jot down the best parts about it. If there are negative things, write them down in a different column. Let your mind expand into blue sky thinking. What would be your ideal bedtime ritual?

To help you find your magic number, I've inserted a sleep diary in the blueprint chapter. The blueprint will give you a good idea where you are now, and will help you be more realistic about how much time you really need in bed each night. Note that we're talking about sleep deprivation, not sleep disorders. Issues like sleep apnea and restless legs are medical. *The Flourishing Home* "is not intended to replace your physician!"

The impact can't be ignored, even for the short term, because there are too many long-term consequences. Sleep scientist William Dement said that the "most important predictor of how long you will live" is how well you sleep. The Flourishing Home is flexible on a lot of things, but to generate true physical and mental health and happiness, this one is a must-have!

**Sleep in the Real World**

Now, I'm the first to admit that moving sleep to the top of the priority list can be a challenge. One client with a family history of metabolic disease including diabetes was also the primary breadwinner. Sleep was low on her totem pole. The best intervention I could offer to decrease her risk of medial issues, lower her stress and anxiety, increase her productivity and take off that last ten pounds was sleep.

This entire book is about creating a home that supports your wellness and wellbeing, so let's consider how roadblocks to a restful night can be overcome. To prove how serious I am about this point, I'm going to share some of the torment that arrived in my life along with my firstborn. I deeply believed in the Ferber Method's recommendation that babies sleep in cribs. So deeply, in fact, that I waited until my son fell asleep then crawled out of his room! Nearly every time, he poked his head up just as I reached the door. The process of soothing him to sleep began again. I quickly became so exhausted that I shook and shivered.

As the birth of my second son approached, I couldn't allow myself to become sleep deprived again. My tactics were very different. I closed the door to my bedroom, turned the ceiling fan on high then covered my head with pillows to block out any sounds that might send me rushing down the hall to the baby's room. Can anyone say, "Heaping pile of guilt?" No matter how awful it felt to do those things, I wanted to be the best mom I could be so sleep was a high priority.

Nearly two years later, my daughter was born. I again tried something different. This time I adopted a whole new philosophy. I needed sleep and she needed to be soothed, so she slept nearby. Nighttime nursing was easier, and eventually she transitioned to her own bed. This experience was by far the least stressful. It worked for her, it worked for me…and we both woke refreshed and well rested!

When searching for answers, find what works for you. Don't allow tradition or textbooks to force you to do things that just don't work. The mother of an autistic boy, for example, got her best sleep in her son's room. Although she and her husband strongly valued being in the same bed together, she was able to soothe her son more quickly if she was in his room. Since both spouses prioritized sleep, they created their Flourishing Home by finding what was best for their family.

Sometimes the answer comes from being flexible. Mary wanted to tuck her kids into bed, mentally prepare for the next day, take a candlelit bath, read for fifteen minutes then fall into hours and hours of peaceful, uninterrupted sleep. That might happen when the moon is in the Seventh House and Jupiter aligns with Mars. Meanwhile, she can pick one or two things from that list every night. Some evenings she'll approach perfection; most nights she'll enjoy one or two. No matter what, though, she'll always get at least a few of the things that truly refuel her body and mind.

### Sleep Tools for All Ages

In the first part of this chapter, we learned that your private retreat should have everything you need at hand. The scented candle, the comfy chair and the pretty view are all tools you use to refresh, relax and recharge. The same is true of the place where you sleep. All the tools you need for a full night's rest should be right there.

Bedding is a valuable tool that's more than just the mattress and box spring. Consider purchasing the best linens you can afford. Even when it's dark, your skin will contact the sheets at many points. Comb spun cotton is cooler and more comfortable than a scratchy polyester. Be mindful of the age of your pillows and mattress. Both should support your body while having enough give to accommodate your joints and curves. As soon as you notice any discomfort, replace them.

Your central air system is another tool that ensures complete rest. People fall asleep more quickly and stay asleep longer in cool environments. Temperatures between 58 and 75 degrees Fahrenheit are best. Combine the air conditioner with ceiling or floor fans for maximum energy efficiency.

**Bedside Tools**

To promote restful sleep, consider keeping some additional tools near your bed. A journal to capture your racing thoughts, ear plugs to block out a spouse's snoring, a night mask to eliminate every bit of light, an extra blanket to avoid a midnight trip to the closet, or an aroma diffuser to send you into blissful dreams might save the night for you!

One of the best things you can do to ensure sound sleep is to be diligent about light sources. Even the glow of a digital alarm clock can impair sleep cycles. Keep your environment as dark as possible. Purchase the most effective window treatments, turn the clock toward the wall, and cover any blinking digital readouts with electrical tape.

TVs and computers put out a relatively strong amount of light and shouldn't be in your sleep area. The programs and content they offer are distracting to your mind and disturb your emotions. And don't even think about having a cell phone in the room. Put it away...far away!

These tools and tactics should be considered for every sleeping environment in the Flourishing Home, even the children's rooms. *Pediatrics* magazine recently reported a link between childhood obesity and sleep deprivation. And, of course, a sleepy child won't perform as well at school.

While I worked with Corrie, we worked for a bit in her children's rooms. It was time well spent! Her daughter told me how one particular piece of her décor upset her. Every night, a garland hung around the window treatments cast eerie shadows on the wall. The remedy was easy. We moved the garland from the window and draped it over the door. No more spooky shadows!

## Home Altars

Oh, boy, suddenly we're looking at another word that needs a definition. *Altar* might seem like a heavy hitter on the spirituality scale, but don't be scared! Even if this seems to be a totally new concept for your Flourishing Home, chances are you probably already have at least a few groupings that look or function like an altar.

So what the heck do I mean by *altar?* At its core, it's a focal point. It serves to bring your attention to a specific thought, feeling, goal, person or place. One common example is the shelf that holds pictures of your family and mementos from trips you've taken together. The mantel dedicated to your most treasured knickknacks is another, along with the corner table that displays your favorite keepsakes.

"What?" I hear you mumble. "My bookshelf is an altar? My family photos are… offerings?"

Well, yes and no. Any space where you've gathered a group of objects that hold meaning for you has the *characteristics* of an altar. Although you certainly don't worship any of the things you place there, the objects have a special purpose…a deeply meaningful and even spiritual purpose! So, in a way, they are offerings to your spirit. The group feeds, or refuels, your mind and your soul. It makes you feel good and helps you remember pleasant times and beautiful places. I can think of no better word than altar for that kind of spiritual refueling!

Areas like these are focal points for you, your family, and sometimes your friends and other guests. The groupings you've deliberately placed there make a statement about your personal values or your family's values. Since this is another of those things that are intensely personal, the ways altars are set up can change dramatically from one person to another. As always, what works for you will define your altar.

The Flourishing Home might have personal altars for any or all of the residents, a family altar, a home altar, or any combination. Many households have altars that were set up unconsciously. When you become aware of your altars and their meaning in your life, you place those pleasant thoughts and feelings directly in your conscious view. You resonate more deeply with what you believe and enjoy.

Corrie, for example, found this conscious awareness very helpful. Once she became aware of the spiritual aspects of home altars, she tweaked her primary altar so that it more accurately reflected her family. An animal figurine she felt personally connected to represented herself. A memento from her husband's passionate hobby stayed on the altar alongside the statue of a family. The one change she made was to remove the guilt burden knickknack. This simple action clarified the altar's meaning: family connection and the pleasure of doing things together.

**Moving into View**

Look at your shelves, fireplace mantel and desktop.

- Have you already set up unconscious alters?
- What does each of these altars represent?
- How can you make adjustments to fully honor and respect what each altar represents?

Altars provide a physical place to meditate, pray, reflect on deeply held values, recite mantras, repeat affirmations, and examine our convictions. They can trigger inner wisdom, expand patience, and integrate our life roles. They help us heal and recall the priorities of our souls. They can be a place where we ask for guidance or a focal point for our thoughts and prayers. No matter how an altar works for you, it's an important part of your Flourishing Home.

## Finding Symbols

Now that you're comfortable with the concept, let's dig a little deeper. When you set up a personal, family or home altar, what you're really doing is working with symbols. A symbol is anything that represents an idea, a process or a person. A butterfly might represent happiness. The tassel from a college graduate's cap can represent success. A gold ring might stand for a spouse. Simple enough, right?

As with many of the other simple things we've explored in *The Flourishing Home,* symbols are incredibly powerful. Experts believe that the subconscious mind is strongly influenced by symbols. The meanings we find in different objects are created by when and how the object was acquired, how and why it was used, and sometimes how long it's been in our possession.

**Creating with the Subconscious**

Set your timer for between ten and twenty minutes. Grab an empty basket or box and walk through your home. Without thinking, gather items that resonate to you. Just react on a subconscious level... if it warms your heart or makes you smile, tuck it in the basket! When the timer goes off, look at the objects. Taken together, what do they say?

Set the basket aside for a week. When you can be quiet for a few minutes, look at the objects again. What message, theme or statement does the grouping offer you now?

That's why a father can donate a fifty-dollar power tool to charity without a second thought while treasuring the twenty-nine cent plastic dinosaur that used to be his son's favorite toy. A teenager might take better care of a stuffed animal left over from childhood than the latest MP3 player. Grown siblings often have to carefully divide a deceased parent's possessions to ensure that every son and daughter receives something meaningful...something of spiritual rather than financial value.

What might seem decorative to a visitor can be a powerful reminder that tells a personal story, brings back fond memories, or stands for personal victories. My husband's passion has always been soccer. I met him on a soccer field and now, thirty years later, he continues to play whenever he gets the chance. One of his most beloved possessions is a green bottle with a faded label. A teammate gave it to him after he scored three goals in his first game. While I see an object that desperately pleads to be relocated to the recycling bin, he recalls a first milestone and a victory shared with teammates.

The bottle has been joined by our sons' first pairs of soccer cleats along with pictures of the boys on the field. The collection speaks to the family's past, present and future, and the shared love of a single sport. Although my husband didn't consciously create an altar, the grouping makes a statement that's more than the sum of the things. It's about a shared passion, the relationship between father and son, and the pleasure they get from playing soccer.

When grouped together, symbolic items can influence your life more than your conscious thoughts. By deliberately selecting certain objects we honor celebrations, remember our family relationships, mark special occasions, enhance life transitions, and reflect on rites of passage. No matter what you value or how few objects you use, the power of your altar is unlimited.

Altars are physical statements about highly personalized and internalized goals like love, abundance, fertility, courage, faith and creativity. They can be installed anywhere...in the corner of the tub, inside a desk drawer, or as part of your garden. A small table, a mirror set face-up on a dresser, or a shadow box can become your altar. One client cleaned out her unused fireplace so the alcove could be set up as a family altar. An unused closet or that tiny extra bedroom can be entirely dedicated to important spiritual concepts.

Altars can be as public or as private as you want. Because they're so personal, they're often set up in the bedroom. Family altars frequently appear in living rooms. An altar in the kitchen will honor the sacrament food provides for the body. They're truly one of the easiest and most powerful tools in your Flourishing Home kit. Use them intentionally to enhance your home's energy and focus the priorities dear to your soul!

**Inner Space**

When objects with personal meaning are gathered together, they make a statement, broadcast a wish, support a belief, point toward a goal, embody an ideal, act as a reminder, or even celebrate a special person or event.

**Favorite Things**

Walk through your home and look around. What objects symbolize something significant? Consider the different environments you pass through outside your home like your work, where you shop regularly, and where your children go to school. What objects there represent something other than the physical purpose they serve?

## The Flourishing Home Gives Back

During the discovery phase of Wellness Walkthroughs, I always ask my clients about activities they want to do more often. Nearly all mention refueling activities like meditation, arts and crafts, or volunteering.

Giving back is definitely a refueling activity. Even though it takes time and effort, charitable work reflects how deeply we're connected to everyone on Earth. It only takes a small amount of time, effort or skill to make a real change in someone's life. Being able to offer that to others is truly something to be grateful for. Gratitude is one of our primary fuels!

My volunteer efforts have spanned every stage of my life. During my college years, I took underprivileged children camping and participated in fundraising efforts for Camp Wildcat. As a young mother, I started a backpack program for foster kids. Over a two-year period we donated roughly 500 backpacks filled with personal items that helped the children settle into their new homes. Now volunteering is a family affair. Last year we harvested and donated hundreds of pounds of peaches from our backyard for America's Grow a Row program.

Volunteering often reflects something spiritual. The activities we choose reflect our internal value system. My desire to help underprivileged kids and adults motivated my efforts. Other people who participate in volunteer projects sometimes take pictures of the final results. Every day they can relive the pleasurable memories created by the feeling of giving during mission tours, project vacations, and volunteering at a local charity.

No matter where you choose to donate your time and effort, you're building a feeling of gratitude for everything you have in your own life. Our impact in the world positively impacts our minds, bodies and spirits. In the Flourishing Home, giving back is a brilliant way to enhance your wellness and wellbeing!

**Takeaway**: Spiritual refueling in the Flourishing Home will move you emotionally, reignite your passions, and recharge your mind and soul.

# CHAPTER SEVEN

# THE SENSES OF PLACE

*I*magine starting your day in a way that gently awakens all your senses…the aroma of coffee tugs you from slumber and the alarm clock loads a morning playlist of your favorite upbeat songs. You pad into the bright yellow kitchen to pour yourself a hot cup of coffee or tea before taking your newspaper to the light-filled deck. The warmth of the sun's rays and the chirping birds provide company as you gather your thoughts about the upcoming day. After a few minutes you head to the bathroom and shower with an invigorating peppermint and rosemary body wash. Back in your dressing area, your morning playlist continues as you slip into crisply pressed clothes. Your day is underway.

Sounds delightful, yes? Before you say that kind of scenario is out of reach, I'm going to challenge about the way you think about your home. Take a moment, right now, to ask yourself how hard it could be to work with natural elements, color, sound, touch and scent in your house. You control all areas of your Flourishing Home, so you can make these elements work for you.

## The Senses of Your Flourishing Home

What is the sense of place in the Flourishing Home? To find out, mix a dash each of architect, environmental psychologist, music therapist, aromatherapist, human behaviorist, scientist, interior decorator, Feng Shui consultant and physician together… and congratulations! You've just become the expert on your home's senses of place.

Your connection with nature as well as with the colors, smells, textures and sounds of your home is somewhat intangible. It's something you feel rather than something you can measure. Since that connection is abstract, it's often difficult to define; setting up fixed rules for it is nearly impossible. Yet, when the right elements come together, they change your house from a physical structure into an authentically rich home. A little focus on the senses of the place where you live will considerably enhance your wellness and wellbeing.

Like so many other aspects of the Flourishing Home, the senses of place are highly individual. The connection to each element discussed in this chapter will mean different things to different people. Since you're a person who grows and changes over the years, your connections to each of these senses will also change over time. No matter where you are right now, simple elements of your home environment will foster authentic lives for you and the other people under your roof.

## Nature

When I was a child, I always felt sad when I visited a zoo. The caged animals lived in sterile environments back then, and a bear curled up in the corner of a room with plain walls and a glass partition didn't seem right. Nowadays, zoo enclosures mimic different natural environments. Animals housed in these kinds of habitats fare much better, in terms of their wellness and wellbeing, than those caged in sterile environments.

While we aren't zoo attractions (well, all right, most of us aren't), humans also fair better when they have access to a natural environment. During the discovery phase of my work, I ask clients two important questions: What is your favorite spot in your home? Why? The answers have a common theme.

*My favorite spot is at the kitchen table because I can look out into the yard.* This client enjoyed a view over an open field with the edge of a forest visible in the distance.

*My favorite spot is the little sitting alcove because I can catch sight of passing deer.* This window looked out into the garden.

*My favorite spot is on the back deck on a beautiful day because I can watch the kids playing.* The view from the second-storey deck overlooked an open field that served as the home's backyard.

My next question is always: What three things would you do to your home if the sky was the limit? These answers also follow a common pattern.

*I would get new window treatments that are easier to open and close so I could look outside.* This client lived in a detached home.

*I would have a backyard.* This answer was provided by a client who lived in a townhouse.

My own favorite spot is in front of a second-storey window in my home. The house sits atop a gently sloping front yard, so that particular window overlooks a neighboring pond and meadow. Rolling mountains in the background complete the pretty picture. The one drawback is a major highway that runs between us and the mountains. The sounds of the highway can be heard at my house. Alas, nothing is perfect…but the view is so beautiful it almost makes up for the noise!

Reading from my own blue sky wish list, I would pick up our home and rotate it 45 degrees to allow more natural light into the house. I would also replace our family room windows with oversized French doors that open into the backyard. The doors would also provide a better view from various places inside the home, especially from the family room couch.

The one aspect all these desires have in common is an increased connection to natural elements. An emerging field of architecture and design deals with this innate need, one that we've intuitively sought for centuries. It's called biophilic design, which is the love of life or the love of living systems. At its core is the belief that people have a basic need for contact with nature. Proponents say that our physical and mental wellbeing "remains highly contingent on contact with natural environment which is a necessity rather than a luxury for achieving lives of fitness and satisfaction…."

Most of you know that more and more builders are valuing environmentally responsible design, construction strategies, and a collection of practices that guide green or LEEDS (Leadership in Energy and Environmental Design) techniques. Biophilic design addresses the physical, psychological and social consequences of the relationship between humans and nature. By reaching beyond organic and energy efficient, it locates the soul of green design.

Studies have examined biophilic principals in medical environments, healthcare, the workplace, childhood development, community function and more. Natural light and a view onto natural areas decreases stress, increases emotional wellbeing, decreases pain, and improves medical outcomes. The Pebbles Project, a research initiative into how design impacts healthcare, is creating more efficient and effective healing environments. The health and wellbeing of patients, staff and visitors is improved by matching tranquil environments that absorb noise with natural light and access to nature.

In the workplace, biophilic design decreases absenteeism and increases productivity. Retail sales can increase as much as 40% just by enhancing the amount of daylight inside a store. Learning environments that incorporate biophilic elements foster better test scores, increase learning rates, generate better behavior, and enhance focus. Corporations, organizations and institutions are adopting biophilic design elements because they offer economic benefits. The same benefits can be applied to the Flourishing Home!

**Biophilic Favorites**

- What are some of your favorite spots in your home?
- How much natural sunlight reaches your favorite spot?
- What natural elements are present?

## Mindful Responses

I always find it helpful to understand the why and how of things rather than blindly follow someone's edict. Why and how does the biophilic response make a difference? Why is the biophilic response important in our homes? To discover the answers, look no further than your own body.

Our nervous systems allow us to hear, smell, touch and see our environments. Most people are aware of the fight-or-flight response, the reaction generated by the sympathetic nervous system. There's another branch called the parasympathetic nervous system. Since it's responsible for all the things the body does when we're relaxed, it has been called the "rest and digest" function. When we interact with nature, the system is triggered more strongly. The results are better body function, improved concentration, decreased stress and irritability, and reduced sympathetic activity (the fight-or-flight response).

The rest and digest function is as basic to all humans as the fight-or-flight response. Biophilic design takes this into account with its concept of *prospect and refuge*. Long ago, our ancestors often chose to rest in spots that were higher than the surrounding terrain. This allowed them to gather the best information on prospects like game and other food sources. The perches also kept them safe…they offered *refuge*. Not surprisingly, the same characteristics often crop up when clients talk about their favorite places inside their homes: in front of a window with an expansive view!

With this idea of prospect and refuge in mind, consider how you move through your home during each day and each season. I'll bet that in summer you gravitate to places of greater prospect like an airy, open porch or deck. During winter months, you probably gravitate to places of greater refuge like a cozy fireplace or a deeply cushioned couch. Your response isn't limited to the view through your window, either. Just like those zoo animals, people enjoy better wellness and wellbeing when provided with things that mimic natural elements. Hospital patients who stayed in rooms decorated with pictures of nature had better medical outcomes than those who looked at abstract art or no artwork at all.

**Elements of Nature**

When incorporating nature into your home environment, be creative. Potted plants are a no-brainer. Add water features, aquariums, or a mini-Zen garden to each room. Spread plush area rugs in moss green or ocean blue. Replace the seating in your breakfast nook with park benches or hang a mobile with colorful origami birds from the ceiling.

Naturally occurring patterns trigger the same kinds of responses that help you relax, release stress, and begin to heal. The crystals formed by a snowflake, the rings of a tree trunk, the spirals inside a nautilus shell, and the ripples on the surface of a pond all provide positive benefits. If you're drawn to geometric patterns, know that they've been shown to cause anxiety in some people. Stick with the softer organic patterns and use geometric ones sparingly.

To enhance your wellness and wellbeing, pay attention to the patterns you choose for upholstery, bed linens and art. Consider representational artwork, ornamentation, organic forms and natural materials. Hang pictures of trees, fields, water and flowers on your walls and even on the refrigerator. Use decorating elements that mimic shells, leaves, and trees. Select furniture with flowing shapes over geometric ones; have wood grains or stone surfaces visible in different areas of your home.

Anything that increases your exposure to nature counts as biophilic design. Open a window at night or prop the door open for a few minutes on a cool spring morning. Soothe yourself to sleep with a recording of whale songs or pave your front walkway with gravel that will crunch under your feet. Turn a cramped bathroom into a steamy jungle by hanging air plants everywhere. Every adjustment supports your health and productivity along with your intellectual and spiritual wellbeing. Enhance your connection to nature and you'll enhance your connection to peace!

One of the most critical aspects of nature and the home environment is exposure to natural light. A detailed explanation of hormones and the sleep-wake cycle is found in chapter six. For now, you only need to know that natural light affects our daily cycle of hormones. Serotonin is linked to our mood and is a big player in seasonal affective disorder (SAD), what most of us call the winter blahs. Melatonin is used by our bodies to regulate sleep. When these hormones are out of balance, our sleep-wake pattern is disturbed.

You might think that switching to bright bulbs will help, but sunlight is very different from artificial light. Any changes that allow more light into your home are critical. Do note that natural light should produce as little glare as possible. Place your furniture carefully and use window treatments that regulate temperature while allowing natural light to come in. You'll reap health benefits that will make your body feel better; your environment will also feel better to you. Better light will also enhance your productivity for all the tasks you need to accomplish in your Flourishing Home.

## Attributes of Biophilic Design

As you adjust the different areas in your home with an eye toward enhancing the natural elements, keep these ten key points in mind:

Dynamic natural light: Light that changes according to the rhythms of your twenty-four hour day as well as the seasons. Patterns of brightness and shadow, along with a little sparkle, relieve stress and mental fatigue. Eliminate glare. Natural ventilation: Air movement, changes in temperature, airborne scents. Humans don't thrive in closed environments!

1. Access to open and or moving water: Visual, acoustic or symbolic. Water is a universal symbol of life.

2. Spontaneous interaction with nature.

3. Sensory connection to nature: Physical, visual or material connections between the interior and nature.

4. Complexity and order: The relationship of variety and intricacy within underlying natural order. Silk road mosques and Incan stonework are good examples of how our innate reaction to the geometry of natural forms is triggered.

5. Mystery: The desire to explore, discover, and learn from the complexities of nature.

6. Prospect and refuge: The safety of home balanced with the opportunities available in a vista.

7. Fundamental natural form: Anything organic that demonstrates rhythm, proportion, repetition, symmetry or gradients.

8. Local natural materials: Connect the site to the building and its interior spaces.

When asked about her blue sky wishes, Susan responded by saying "a big yard." Well, this idea was as blue as my wish to rotate my home 45 degrees. Susan lives in a townhouse, so incorporating a vista, views and natural elements was a wee bit trickier. The middle unit town home only had views to the outside via the front and back balconies and one additional window off the dining area. Her obstacles were real but not insurmountable. Among our idea sparks was to move the furniture at the heart of her home (the living area and kitchen) so that she could see out the window and over the balcony.

A simple flip of a comfy chair to the other side of the room took no money and five minutes to implement but for the client, the tweak brought more nature into her visual environment. In addition, the insight that resulted from her blue sky wish inspired her to enhance her balcony environments. Potted plants, can-

**Create Your Own Savanna**

Look at the views offered by your windows. How can they be enhanced? Consider changing window treatments, creating miniature courtyard gardens, adding wind chimes, hanging a birdhouse, or setting up planters or lawn art inside the view.

**For Every Season**

- What is your favorite spot inside your home during each season?
- What are your favorite spots early in the morning, during the day, at twilight and after dark?

dles and some comfortable chairs were added to the front balcony. For the back balcony, we reworked the window treatments to create darkness during her sleep times. The shades could be easily opened to let in natural light and fresh air. The simple aha! moment that came when she realized her desire for a yard could be translated successfully inside her townhouse helped her home flourish.

## A Rainbow of Color

Whenever I offer presentations on The Flourishing Home, the question of color inevitably comes up. Right now I'm asking you to take off your architect and environmental psychologist hats. Grab your interior designer swatch book, don your Feng Shui consultant cloak, and scribble in your behavioral psychologist notebook. We're going to learn how color impacts our wellness and wellbeing!

First a note to my Feng Shui friends. Bless you for deciphering the principles of that system. You know how aspects of life like career, family, and marriage coordinate with natural elements like earth, wood, water and fire in a single room or an entire building. You factor in the placement of different doorways and windows while calculating the room's orientation to the points of the compass.

Oh, and of course there are different schools of Feng Shui. Classical forms include the Xuan Kong School or Flying Stars and the Ba Zhai or Eight Mansions. Modern forms include Life Aspirations, Pyramid, Intuitive, Fusion, and Black Hat. Each has its own approach and often the different types offer conflicting ideas from how to live in harmony with nature.

If you think Feng Shui presents some challenging puzzles, don't get me started on interior designers! Their thoughts on how to implement color in a home can be just as varied. Don't use bright colors, use bright colors; don't be monochromatic, monochromatic is soothing... argh! For readers who really want to torture themselves, compare the Feng Shui principles to typical interior decorating philosophies. You won't get far before you discover how few of the ideas agree.

Oh, and did you say you want to be trendy? Turns out there are entire organizations that forecast the hottest color trends for every year. Sometimes their recommendations change each season. Think blues and aqua are hot right now? Just wait; they'll be out in only a few months. Unless your decorating budget allows you to change accessories every season and you have enough spare time to roll new paint almost as quickly as the old coat dries, let's take a breath.

I suggest starting with the simple question "What's your favorite color?" Mine is purple. While the rooms in my home aren't twenty different shades of purple, I use purple accents in my office because the color brings me so much joy. If you're not really sure which colors are your favorite, look in your closet. Pull out your favorite pieces and see which hues show up time and again. Still not sure? Look at pictures of rooms you like in books, magazines and newspapers and on websites. File them together for a few weeks, then spread them out on the floor. I can almost guarantee a certain color or blend of colors will jump out.

In the meantime, put aside all the rules you've ever heard about what colors mean and whether certain ones work together. Reflect on what certain colors mean to you. If the yellow that matches the walls of your grandparents' home bring back pleasant memories and evokes warmth and love, then maybe yellow is a color you want somewhere in your home. If blue makes you feel upbeat because you associate it with happy vacations, by all means put aside the rule that blue is a cool color. The meanings you'll attach to different hues and specific tones are personal. If it works for you, it will be a positive part of your Flourishing Home!

Now, some of you still want a little guidance. There's nothing wrong with using traditional ideas as springboards. The guidelines set by different systems can spark new ways of thinking. I'm therefore listing the common associations made by designers and ancient teachings:

- **Red:** Stimulating, intense, dramatic, passionate
- **Orange:** Friendly, cheerful, creative
- **Yellow:** Warm and welcoming, happy, visible
- **Blue:** Tranquil, serene, open
- **Green:** Earthy, calming, soothing
- **White:** Purity, goodness, freshness
- **Brown:** Earthy, neutral, relaxing, grounding
- **Black:** Sophisticated, authority, power; also dark and depressing

Your color choice will be personal but be mindful of what you want to feel in each room. What mood do you want to set? How can color enhance the mood and feel? The structural and functional elements need to be considered while you're deciding how the walls should be painted and how accessories can play off the primary color scheme.

Sometimes all those choices can feel overwhelming, especially when it comes to color. Some paint companies offer over a hundred shades of white, so finding the ideal shade of blue might be a challenge. Good for you if you have a simpatico decorator at your disposal or if you're already flourishing with the colors currently in your home environment. If you're among those of us who freeze at the thought of a paint brush and a blank wall, don't fret! The Flourishing Home solutions are simple even when it comes to color.

Katherine was confused by a space she wanted to be a heart for the extended family when they gathered during visits. She wanted more color but the many options were paralyzing. Little did she realize that the answers could be found in clues that surrounded her. Questions posed during our walkthrough about favorite artwork, prized knickknacks, and recurring colors in her clothes created a palette of deep jewel tones. Maybe at some point she'll feel comfortable committing a wall to one of the dramatic colors she likes. In the meantime, she pulled together items already on hand.

A selection of candles in ruby red, emerald green, sapphire and amethyst were added to the room. A piece of favored artwork was moved from a spare bedroom to become a focal point of the new heart. She added a few colored frames to her wish list. By tuning into the clues in her environment, she harnessed the power of colors to transform a frustrating space into a welcoming heart that felt authentic to her and others.

A few additional concepts might be helpful as you consider color in your Flourishing Home. First is the idea that colors can be cool or warm. Generally warm colors are ones you consider vivid and energetic. They tend to pop out and can make a room really hop. That's why red is so often used in spaces where you want to entertain; it makes people feel upbeat and increases how much they socialize. Cool colors, on the other hand, feel calm and soothing. They recede in your visual field and draw you into a more introspective mode. Bedrooms are perfect places for cool colors. In this concept, white, black and gray are neutral.

You also can consider whether tints, shades or tones of a specific color should be part of a room's overall scheme. Tints are created by adding more white to a color. Shades are created by adding more black. Mixing gray into a hue creates a different tone. If I were to set up a room that is done completely in purple, I might start with a middle-of-the-road grape for the walls. Adding white gives me something more like lavender for the trim. Adding black provides royal purple for the upholstery while mixing in gray gives me a dusky tone that works well in an area rug.

---

**Idea Spark: DIY Art**

Blank canvas that has already been mounted on frames can be found at your local craft store. Some pieces can be rather large while others are miniature. To discover exactly how a particular color resonates with you, paint the canvas that color and live with it for a while. Move the canvas around inside the room to see how it looks under different kinds of light. You might even find that the canvas provides the perfect splash of color. Yes, you can use it as decor!

---

Finally, you might mix complementary or analogous colors. Complementary colors are complete opposites. They yield a vibrant look but can be difficult to pull off when you're working with large areas. To be safe, restrict your complementary color usage to accessories and small areas. Analogous colors sit next to each other on the color wheel and are very compatible. Analogous colors are what we often see in nature, so this kind of mixture is very pleasing. It's also much easier to work with because you just have to pick two or three that sit side by side on the wheel!

## The Flourishing Aroma

Even the cleanest house can have unpleasant scents. Cooking odors can find their way into the living room. The sweat caught in running shoes can cling to all the clothes in the closet. This is normal, of course. The danger is that over time, the people who live there become numb to the unpleasant odors. A person who lives with three cats, for example, might not notice the litter box smell if it isn't very strong. But a visitor with no cats will notice right away!

Just to be sure you haven't grown numb to your home's aroma, step outside for a moment. Shut the door behind you and breathe deeply a few times. Then go back inside and inhale fully and slowly through your nose. What aromas and odors do you detect?

When you enter a home for the first time, the scents you pick up can shape your perception of the entire house. A pleasant smell is much more likely to make you anticipate a pleasant visit. Walk into a beautifully appointed, obviously clean room with a moldy odor and chances are the smell is all you'll notice! Your visual cues will be overridden by the mildew. Enter a home with a fair share of mess lying about that has a lemony smell and you'll likely overlook the clutter.

Aromatherapy uses essential oils for their impact on wellness and wellbeing. Although aromatherapy has recently become popular, it's actually part of a tradition that began more than two thousand years ago. The Chinese thought that burning aromatic plants as incense created harmony and balance. Egyptian cultures distilled different types of oils from plants and trees. The Greeks thought the effects of perfumes were important to health and psychology; they credited the gods with having provided the knowledge to mankind.

**That Old Scent Magic**

As you go through your day, pause now and again to sniff the air.

- What scents do you associate with positive memories?
- Think about how your home feels during different seasons. Which scents show up during each season?

Couple the long-standing practice of aromatherapy with scientific research and the power of the nose grows. While there's no concrete scientific theory that fully explains why our sense of smell impacts us so strongly, we know that the human nose can recognize 10,000 odors. The scent receptors transfer information to the part of our brain that controls memory and emotion. The limbic system is connected to the pituitary gland and the hypothalamus, both of which release hormones that affect appetite, the nervous system, body temperature, stress levels and concentration. When we stimulate these organs with scents, we encourage the release of certain kinds of hormones.

Olfactory experiences are so important they're making their way into businesses. Realtors have tapped into this power for years by using the aroma of freshly baked cookies to help sell homes. More retailers are attracting and keeping customers through pleasant aromas. Hotels have created signature scents to enhance positive associations for guests. Casinos, spas, fitness centers, convention centers, airports, train stations, theaters and cruise lines also appear on the growing list.

While businesses and organizations are going to rely on the rules laid out by their consultants, your Flourishing Home will reflect your personal scent palate. For me, the aromas of chlorine and banana candy evoke strong responses. Oddly enough, I find the smell of chlorine calming! As a former swimmer, the scent of a pool is comforting. The sickeningly sweet banana candy smell, on the other hand, dredges up awful memories of the antibiotic I had to take for weeks as a child.

Now, I would never infuse my home with the smell of chlorine no matter what it means to me! I'm just using these examples to show how specific my association with each smell is. Most people wrinkle their noses at pool water and take an extra whiff of sweet banana candy. Make sure you know what kind of mood the aroma you're considering will evoke for you. Its power to revive an emotion or memory is that strong!

---

### Idea Spark: Your Signature Scent

Consider creating a signature aroma for your home. You can do this by selecting a plug-in air freshener for the spaces where you entertain friends and any place where your family gathers. You can also buy several essential oils at your local organic grocer to blend in a diffuser. If you're so inclined, you can develop different aromas for different seasons.

---

## A Scent for Every Space

To influence your Flourishing Home's effect on wellness and wellbeing, remember that different aromas can evoke different responses. Each scent is believed to stimulate different parts of the brain and lead to different reactions. Peppermint, for example, has been found to decrease food cravings by 90 percent. People who sniff peppermint throughout the day eat 2,800 calories fewer a week…almost a pound! Studies found that people who inhaled a peppermint scent every two hours ate 1,500 to 2,700 fewer calories per week. Banana, green apple and vanilla had similar effects.

Science supports the direct effect inhaling odors has on the satiety center of the brain. This area tells your body when you've had enough to eat. If you're looking to maintain a healthy weight and struggle with keeping the best caloric balance, the availability of peppermint odors in the kitchen just might tip the scale in your favor. The use of floral scents in the kitchen can counteract the appetite-stimulating aromas of food. A vase of lilies moved to the table after a meal can halt the body's reaction to stimulating aromas.

---

### Idea Spark: Spreading the Special Scent

Consider all the different ways you can incorporate positive aromatic influences. Lighting a scented candle at the end of the work day can help you relax. Lavender bath oil will soothe your mind while the warm water soothes your body. Aromatic diffusers, organic room sprays, essential oils dabbed on a potpourri or a drawer sachet will integrate pleasant smells throughout your Flourishing Home.

---

Inhaling a fragrance such as lavender can reduce stress, lift depression, hasten a good night's sleep, soothe your soul, or restore your energy level. Use energizing and soothing aromas in your spiritual refueling area to maximize the space's impact.

Since aromatherapy is already helping office workers stay alert while doing repetitive mental tasks, you can apply the same logic to information hubs in your home. Try invigorating scents at your command central and bill paying hubs to maximize your efficiency during these tasks.

As usual, knowing how different systems think about aromas can help you build your own foundation or spark new ways to mix and match scents. Here are some general guidelines culled from different aromatherapists.

- **Lavender:** Stress relief
- **Lemon:** Stress relief, combat fatigue, lift spirits, energize
- **Orange:** Stress relief
- **Patchouli:** Stress relief, combat fatigue

- **Vanilla:** Stress relief, appetite suppressant
- **Ylang Ylang:** Stress relief, appetite suppressant
- **Chamomile:** Stress relief, relaxation
- **Peppermint:** Improve memory, appetite suppressant, enhance alertness
- **Rosemary:** Improve memory, enhance clarity
- **Ginger:** Combat fatigue
- **Eucalyptus:** Evoke positive mood
- **Bergamot:** Stress relief, combat fatigue, lift depression

## Alive with Sound

The sounds of nature—birds chirping in the summer, the quiet sifting of snow falling, the rustle of leaves in autumn, the wind and rain of spring—surround our homes. We have little control over them but generally they're viewed as positive. Also out of our control is the noise of everyday life—a neighbor's leaf blower or the shrieks of children playing. Those we encounter in the workplace or businesses we visit are also out of our control.

We do have control over electronic sources, especially our choice of music. Psychologists have proven that music influences us in good and bad ways by altering our moods and emotions. Music can therefore be a powerful element of the Flourishing Home, a tool that can enhance our wellness and wellbeing. Once you've engaged your blue sky thinking on how you want your home to sound, it's time to utilize tools that will enhance some sounds and minimize others. You have a lot more control than you might think.

Biophilic sounds often aren't a big part of a condo or apartment or townhouse's environment, but that can be easily fixed. Place a birdfeeder or nesting box next to a window or by the door leading out to your balcony to attract songbirds. A miniature fountain creates the soothing patter of water in any room, and tiny wind chimes hung near an air conditioning vent will remind you of lazy summer afternoons spent lounging in a backyard. There are even clocks that use the songs of different birds to announce every hour!

Natural sounds are just the beginning. A gong placed near the dining room table can gently bring the family together for a shared meal. Tibetan singing bowls, brass bowls you play by rubbing the lip with a wood peg, can focus your thoughts before you pay bills. Bells hung on the knob of your exterior door can send a pleasant tone throughout the house whenever you come home.

To deal with negative sounds like the compressor on your refrigerator or the swooshing dishwasher, try ambient sound machines. You can buy ones that replicate natural sounds like waves or rain, or you can set the switch to white noise that covers up the sound of the machines. Annoying sounds from the laundry area can be muffled by lining the back of the door with a thick tapestry. The electronic buzz of a television or sound system can be minimized by housing the units inside cabinets.

---

**The Sound Environment**

Become mindful of the noises and sounds of your environment. Consider sounds that seep into the house from outside as well as the noises made by various appliances.

- Which are present naturally?
- What noises occur throughout the day?
- Which change depending on the season?
- Do you prefer a quiet environment?
- Which of these are positive? Which are negative?

Once you've located the positive sounds in your Flourishing Home, you can bring those same sounds into different areas. Once you're mindful of the negative sounds, you can make changes to decrease or eliminate them.

---

With only a few simple tools and a little investment of your time, you'll create a sound environment that truly supports your overall wellness and wellbeing. In the Flourishing Home, nothing is more important!

## Make Your Flourishing Home Sing

Music can be used for amusement, to enhance a dinner party, or be the background for an evening spent relaxing on the couch. It can revive and refresh your mood in the morning when you need a bit more stimulation to prepare for your day. Music can also deepen sensation. Film soundtracks do this all the time by dubbing sad music to heighten an emotional moment or using discordant, scary music to enhance a thrill.

Music can also create a diversion...it can distract the mind from unpleasant thoughts and can discharge emotions by purging negative thoughts. By filling the silence, music can decrease our experience of pain while we heal. During intensely mental work like learning a new skill or doing taxes, classical music will slow the heartbeat and pulse rate, improve concentration, decrease blood pressure and speed the rate at which we learn.

---

**A Musical Mood**

- What's on your music menu today?
- What sounds do you want... silence, nature, a symphony?
- What do you wish to accomplish right now, and how can music help?

---

Lastly, and perhaps most important for your Flourishing Home, research proposes that music can provide solace. The right tone to a musical composition can reconnect us to something we've lost or link us to a shared emotion or experience. If you've had a lot of arguments lately with a spouse or a troubled teen, select a song both of you enjoy. Before taking up the conversation again, sit together for a few minutes and listen deeply. When the song is over, take a deep breath and look each other in the eye. You might be surprised how much more productive your new conversation becomes!

Here's the big bonus: How you use music in your Flourishing Home isn't limited to a single goal. You can apply the benefits to several goals at once! Happy music can divert, entertain and revive you in the morning and in the evening. Soulful music can provide solace and encouragement while discharging negative emotions when you face too many chores or after a tough day at work. The power of music is yours. Use it to reap wellness and wellbeing in all areas of your life!

As you set up different listening stations, remember that there is no formula for matching music to mood or wellness and wellbeing goals. The pieces you'll find relaxing, soothing, invigorating or deeply moving will be highly personal. If you're a fan of heavy metal, all those thrashing guitars can help dissipate negative emotions. If you're not a fan of grunge, the same songs can impact you negatively. That's why so many parents are driven mad by their teenagers' favorite bands!

What you'll listen to in different areas of your Flourishing Home will depend on who's going to listen and what each person likes and dislikes. The styles you prefer will also change with your mood. A track that motivates you on Tuesday can feel boring on Friday. The classical piece that soothes you in the evening might put you right back to sleep when it's time to get up in the morning. Just as music affects moods, your moods will affect your choices. You might even find that your selection reflects your internal state of mind more accurately than your conscious mind knows!

---

### Idea Spark: A Flourishing Playlist

By teaching group fitness classes over the last twenty-five years, I've learned about the power of music to make or break a class. A great beat combined with the right tempo and lyrics can take the energy level through the roof. Participants leave feeling empowered and positive. Technology makes it easy to create and adjust custom playlists.

Inventory your music library. Create a wellness and wellbeing playlist. Consider whether you want different ones for the morning and evening. Would you like one specifically to release stress? Another to listen to while you engage in mentally taxing work? A get happy collection? One that works out your daily frustration? The possibilities are endless!

The technology available to create your music playlist or music menus makes this as easy as a touch of a button. Burn songs from CDs onto your iPod for personal playlists. Download tunes onto your computer and let them play in the background while you work. Create a music menu to play on the stereo during family meals or even while you do chores. Considering how easy this is, there really isn't any reason not to!

---

## That Special Touch

One more sense is very important in your Flourishing Home…the sense of touch. The textures you use throughout your home aren't something most people consider but they really have a powerful impact on your wellness and wellbeing. The texture of an object is found mostly on its surface area. The fullness of the texture can be enhanced by the object's weight and balance. For example, a knife handle that's smooth might not be comfortable if it's too heavy or if the blade isn't balanced.

The same kinds of things will affect the sense of touch. Whenever your hand or skin connects with the upholstery, wallpaper, tablecloth or kitchen counter, your body and mind react. Even when only your eyes take in a texture, you still respond to the interplay of light and shadow created by the surface. Touch, therefore, works in much the same way as music, sound and scent. We have a physical response that brings up memories, triggers emotions, and enhances our wellness and wellbeing.

If there's one person who knows the importance of texture, it's my son Tristan. As a baby and a toddler, and still now as a blossoming teenager, he's been drawn to soft things. As a baby, he would comfort himself with a tattered cotton t-shirt. As a toddler, he checked the texture of clothes before putting them on. Like a chef tasting a dish, Tristan tests the "taste" of texture. Today he's partial to a particular set of sheets and pillowcases. They are in fact the softest sheets in the house!

Now that we're talking about texture, look around your home. It's everywhere! Even if it's the same color, the upholstery on your couch might be different from what was used on the chairs. The arms of most chairs are a completely different texture than the seat. Wainscoting provides a much more interesting texture than walls that are plain. Even paint can be smooth, rippled like an orange peel, or made bumpy by faux finishes.

Every kind of texture creates a positive or negative impact. And now we're really into personal likes and dislikes. A grainy granite-like finish might delight one person with strong biophilic tendencies but will irritate a person who likes crisp finishes! The industrial metal and glass furniture popular in lofts will make one person feel avant-garde while a visitor might find it cold and impersonal. There really is no all-purpose guide for working with textures in your home. Whatever makes you flourish is the right choice!

## Texture Basics

The largest areas to consider are pretty obvious. The texture of a room's walls can be adjusted with paint, faux finishes or wainscoting. Wallpaper can provide you with everything from a smooth, cloth-like texture to a coarse seagrass surface. Textiles hung in strategic places can add nubby wool, plush velvet or the thick comfort of alpaca. While working with the walls, think a bit about the ceiling. A smooth, blank space is traditional but you might like the ornate plasterwork or the punched tin plating that was popular decades ago. A subtle faux finish on the ceiling can make a room stand out.

The floor is another primary area. It's one of the biggest spaces in each room; it also can pull together different elements inside the room. Hardwood or laminate now come in textures ranging from glossy smooth to a rough, weathered feel. There's even a midrange choice that replicates hand-finished planks; this gives you the smoothness of a glossy finish while keeping a more natural visual texturing. Carpeting ranges from formal Berber style to informal shag. Throw rugs can be sturdy braided rag rugs or finely woven silk and wool.

---

### Idea Spark: Wall Texture

- Wallpaper comes in a variety of textures but you don't have to commit to papering an entire room. Paper just one wall to create a special accent.
- Paint can also have texture. Try a bumpy granite for a boy's room. A thick orange peel texture works great in a kitchen while a sandy feel adds an outdoor touch to a sunroom.
- You can even move beyond the traditional options. Living walls with real plants are a green alternative to potted plants. Water walls can be created by installing flat, self-enclosed fountains. There's no limit to the ways you can create texture on your walls!

---

Next, of course, is the furniture. Upholstery and the finishing elements on the arms and edges all provide texture. Even a single type of upholstery can provide a wide range of options. Leather furniture, can be thick and rugged, soft and yielding, or buttery smooth. Silks and cottons can be backed with sturdy canvas or further textured with embroidery. The new generations of vinyl are quite versatile and can mimic everything from calfskin to crocodile!

In the kitchen, you'll want to consider how a texture will function. A butcher block countertop is fantastic for serious cooks, but with heavy use will develop nicks and scars. Concrete countertops are gaining popularity because they're poured in place and can accommodate unusual configurations. They're available in any color you can imagine and are often less expensive than stone. But if the surface isn't finished properly, cleaning can become a real chore.

Marble and granite are great alternatives to laminate in terms of durability and beauty. Nowadays, though, there are plastic laminates that outperform the old wood laminates…and they're much more affordable than stone. Tiles of any type can be installed. You can even get stainless steel or copper countertops to coordinate with that restaurant-grade stove you love so much!

Textures can show up in any part of a room. Drawers can be fronted with wicker, cane or fabric. A so-so nightstand can become spectacular when flat dots of glass are glued down the sides. A simple line of nail heads can outline anything from a couch or dresser to the ottoman.

### Textures in Your Flourishing Home

- What textures show up throughout your Flourishing Home?
- What textures appear in your refueling areas–your personal space, each bedroom, and the hearts?
- What textures can you add or subtract to benefit each area?
- Even in transition areas and hubs, how can the use of texture enhance the space?
- Would a small area rug add warmth to a functional hub?
- Would the removal of carpeting help create a clean, uncluttered feeling for an informal hub?

Cabinet handles, quilts and comforters, doorknobs, throw pillows, lap blankets and artwork can all be selected with texture in mind. Make every contact a pleasurable one inside your Flourishing Home.

**Takeaway:** A Flourishing Home's senses of place can increase your focus, decrease stress, and soothe you into deeper levels of wellness and wellbeing.

# CHAPTER EIGHT

## BLUEPRINTS

*S*o you've read the whole book... or maybe you jumped around and ended up here. No matter how you made it to this point, use this section in whatever way works best for you. You'll find some of the questionnaires, worksheets and inventory checklists I use for Home Wellness and Wellbeing walkthroughs here. These DIY tools will guide you in creating your own Flourishing Home.

This entire chapter is about you, the other people living under your roof, and the friends and extended family members you welcome into your home. Read through all the blueprints to find the ones that really resonate with you. Feel free to use all of them or only a few. The end result will bring clarity and mindfulness to your efforts. It will outline your plan for achieving the changes you want to make.

Some of these blueprints are straightforward. The kitchen inventory groups the tools you already have on hand so you can see what's missing. Some blueprints require a bit more thought. Other blueprints like the Home Mission Statement are open ended. Your response might end up being an essay or a collage of pictures. Enjoy the inspiration each sheet offers as you create a home that supports your happiness, health, and rock-the-world sexy attitude!

## VALUES FOUNDATION BLUEPRINT

Have you ever taken the time to write down your values, interests, hobbies, passions and preferences? By doing so, you become mindful of what's truly important. Your goals, hopes and needs become more concrete. Use this worksheet to create clarity for you and your family.

Assign a section to every person in your household put their names on top. The final section will represent the entire group. Pass the sheet around and have everyone fill in their answers.

Once that's done, have a family meeting so you can fill out the group section together. You'll be able to prioritize everyone's individual needs with the needs and goals of the entire group. You might be surprised at what pops up!

Over time, refer back to this sheet as individuals and as a family. Ask if what you're doing inside the home reflects the most important elements of your life. Is your Flourishing Home supporting those areas? What changes can be made to ensure full and continuous support?

■ Start with your section, then prepare sheets for your family members.

Values _____

_____

_____

Interests_____

_____

_____

Hobbies _____

_____

_____

Passions_____

_____

_____

Preferences _____

_____

## Family Home Mission Statement Blueprint

Tack up a poster board where everyone living in your Flourishing Home can share their thoughts, desires, interests and passions. Encourage them to write, sketch or pin up pictures of anything that sheds lights on what's important to them. Include things such as life purposes, hopes, guiding principles, family phrases, individual philosophies and ambitions.

Let it develop over time and see what evolves. Your home's Mission Statement might spring up naturally from this blueprint. At some point, sit down together and write out a Family Home Mission Statement based on the board. Place the statement somewhere visible so everyone can use it as a touchstone.

Every year, revisit this blueprint and put up a new poster board. You might find that the statement will change only a little over the year. Sometimes, though, a new statement will be very different. By checking in occasionally, you'll keep everyone in your Flourishing Home on track for optimal wellness and wellbeing!

■ Start your Family Home Mission Outline here:

Life purposes _____

_____

Hopes _____

_____

Guiding principles _____

_____

Family phrases _____

_____

Individual philosophies _____

_____

Ambitions _____

_____

Passions _____

_____

Other _____

## ROOM FOUNDATION BLUEPRINT

The Room Foundation Blueprint defines how each area functions in the home. You'll explore what's working well and what might be functioning at less than optimal capacity.

Patterns will emerge throughout your home if your eyes are continually drawn to positive or negative aspects that show up in more than one area. If the comfy pillows in the hearts of your home make you feel safe and relaxed, they might be incorporated into other areas. If piles of paper in transition points and hubs are distracting, maybe it's time to tackle clutter throughout the house.

How does each area of your home function… as a hub or a heart? as a formal transition point? Does any one area work in more than one way? Once you know how each area functions, you can tweak as necessary.

## Closet Detective Blueprint

Whether you're a man or a woman, the clothes you wear say something about you... to yourself! This blueprint helps you figure out what your closet says about you. By looking at your closet through the eyes of a detective, you can glean insights about your likes and dislikes. Apply those to different aspects of your Flourishing Home to further boost your wellness and wellbeing. Start by looking through the clothes hanging on the rods.

- What types of clothes dominate: professional suits, athletic wear, casual shirts?

_____

_____

_____

_____

- What types do you wear most often?

_____

_____

_____

- Do you want to wear a certain type more or less often? What will that shift represent in your life?

_____

_____

_____

- What colors show up most often?

_____

_____

_____

- What textures show up most often?

_____

_____

_____

_____

- What types of shoes are there?

_____

_____

_____

- Does the selection and variety…or lack of variety…reflect different aspects of your personality?

_____

_____

_____

- Are you holding on to clothes you'll never wear again? If so, why?

_____

_____

_____

- Any other thoughts about your clothes?

_____

_____

_____

_____

_____

## For the Littlest Residents Blueprint

Often children's rooms function in many ways. They allow for personal expression and reflection, offer a refuge from the world, refuel through sleep, provide a heart where friends can gather, act as a homework hub, and have closets to help kids start and end their days.

By simplifying the concepts you've read about, your child's personal space can benefit from the Flourishing Home's techniques. Sit down with your children and ask about their bedrooms.

■ Do they sleep well? Does any sound or sight keep them from getting to sleep or staying asleep?

_____

_____

_____

_____

■ Can they do their chores or homework easily there?

_____

_____

_____

_____

■ Do they find it easy to keep their rooms clean? (The clutter checklist works great with kids!)

_____

_____

_____

_____

■ Does the room give them a place where they can think about things?

_____

_____

_____

_____

- Does the room feel like a place where they can have fun and be themselves?

_____

_____

- Is it a place where they can safely meet friends?

_____

_____

- Does it reflect their likes, hobbies, passions?

_____

_____

- What works well for them?

_____

_____

_____

- Is there anything they'd like taken out of their rooms so they have more space or a nicer place to meet with friends?

_____

_____

_____

- Lately have they felt like the color or the things in their room aren't interesting to them anymore?

_____

_____

_____

- What kinds of things in the room make them feel good?

_____

_____

_____

## Bedroom Inventory Blueprint

**Best Possible Bedding**
- Age of mattress?
- Should pillows and/or mattress be refreshed or replaced?

    Pillow _____

    Blankets _____

    Linens_____

    Mattress _____

**Lighting:**
- Shades/window covering _____

**Light sources that will interfere with the sleep cycle:**
- Alarm clock _____
- Electronics _____
- Phones _____

    **Other:**
- Temperature: Generally best between 65 and 72 degrees _____
- Noise_____

    Minimize or eliminate _____

*Tools:*
- Journal to capture racing thoughts
- Ear plugs
- Eye mask
- Lip balm
- Tissues
- Aromatherapy Throw for extra warmth
- Water
- Humidifier

Other_____

_____

_____

## APPRECIATIVE INQUIRY BLUEPRINT

This blueprint is all about things that make you feel good. Anything can end up here! You might list activities or types of entertainment. You'll probably include quite a few personal items because they act as primes, trigger memories, and provide comfort. Right now we're looking for the core of all those elements: How the areas or things or activities make you feel.

- What do you love?

_____

_____

_____

- Which room is your favorite?

_____

- Why is that your favorite?

_____

_____

_____

- Which rooms do you gravitate to for relaxation, for fun, and for family time?

_____

_____

_____

_____

- What, about each room, makes you feel good?

_____

_____

_____

_____

- Do you have a favorite seat? Why?

_____

_____

_____

_____

- What are your five favorite objects in the house? In each room? Why?

_____

_____

_____

_____

_____

_____

- What other homes have you visited that appeal to you? Why?

_____

_____

_____

_____

_____

_____

- What works well in your home?

_____

_____

_____

_____

_____

■ What colors and textures do you gravitate towards?

_____

_____

_____

_____

_____

■ What does each color make you feel?

_____

_____

_____

_____

_____

■ What does each texture make you feel?

_____

_____

_____

_____

_____

■ What kind of lighting do you like for tasks, for relaxation, for visiting with guests?

_____

_____

_____

_____

_____

■ What smells and sounds are positive for you?

_____

_____

_____

_____

_____

_____

■ What are your desires?

_____

_____

_____

_____

_____

_____

_____

■ What motivates you?

_____

_____

_____

_____

_____

Other?

_____

_____

_____

_____

## FLOURISHING HOME GOALS BLUEPRINT

Before you take the first step toward implementing your goals, take a look at each desire, wish and need. It's useless and very frustrating to pursue goals if your budget, time, skills, or the skills of your family aren't up to the task. To make the process go as smoothly as possible, take a few minutes to look over your goals.

- Is each goal listed for my Flourishing Home specific?

_____

_____

_____

_____

_____

_____

- Have I clearly defined the different steps I'll need to achieve that goal?

_____

_____

_____

_____

_____

_____

- Will the final result be measurable? If so, how?

_____

_____

_____

_____

_____

_____

_____

- Will achieving that goal have a positive impact?

_____

_____

_____

_____

_____

- Is the goal realistic?

_____

_____

- Should I set a timeframe to motivate me or will that make me feel pressured?

_____

_____

- Will having achieved the goal help me thrive?

_____

_____

- Will having achieved the goal positively affect other aspects of my wellness, wellbeing, or home environment?

_____

_____

_____

- Is it written down clearly?

_____

_____

_____

_____

- Does everyone else living in the home desire the same thing?

_____

_____

_____

_____

_____

_____

- Is everyone else aware of this goal?

_____

_____

_____

_____

- Am I aware of others' goals regarding wellness, wellbeing, and the home environment?

_____

_____

_____

_____

- Are the home goals posted somewhere?

_____

_____

_____

_____

- Have I shared my goals with people who'll support me?

_____

_____

_____

_____

## YOUR HEART'S DESIRE BLUEPRINT

This is your personal Flourishing Home Blueprint. Ask yourself one question: What activities, if any, do you wish to do but struggle to find the time for?

Keep this question in mind as you fill out the responses. By making your house work for you, you'll enhance your wellness and wellbeing while capturing the time you need to fulfill your heart's desires.

Before you turn to the next blueprint, answer this blue sky question: What would be the best outcome of having read this book?

## PRIMES BLUEPRINT

This blueprint will help you discover the positive primes that are already in your environment, enhance those that are most powerful, and add new ones. For each category listed here, use your blue sky thinking to pull in every person, place, event or thing that might be included. Even if some items already showed up in previous categories, go ahead and list them two or more times.

**Categories:**

- Positive People

_____

_____

_____

_____

_____

- Positive Places

_____

_____

_____

_____

_____

- Positive Memories

_____

_____

_____

_____

_____

■ Positive Symbols

_____

_____

_____

_____

_____

_____

■ Positive Milestones or Events

_____

_____

_____

_____

■ Positive Words or Affirmations

_____

_____

_____

_____

■ Positive Scents

_____

_____

_____

_____

■ Positive Goal Reminders

_____

_____

_____

_____

_____

Now look at the list for each category. Ask yourself:

■ Which of these positive primes already exist in my Flourishing Home?

_____

_____

_____

_____

_____

■ Which of these would I like to have more of?

_____

_____

_____

_____

_____

■ Which primes show up in two or more categories? These are likely more important to you than other primes.

_____

_____

_____

_____

_____

■ Of the primes on my list that are currently not in my Flourishing Home, which ones am I most drawn to?

_____

_____

_____

_____

_____

_____

## Inspiration Reflections Blueprint

Look back at the inspiration boards you created while reading through the previous chapters.

- What themes arose from each board?

_____

_____

_____

_____

- How are they currently reflected in your Flourishing Home?

_____

_____

_____

_____

- Which pieces of your board are missing from your environment?

_____

_____

_____

_____

- Which aspects that already exist do you want more of?

_____

_____

_____

_____

- What kinds of items are placed next to each other?

_____

_____

_____

■ How are the items placed: linearly, overlapped, evenly spaced?

_____

_____

_____

_____

■ Did you choose pieces that were mostly words or mostly pictures?

_____

_____

_____

■ What colors appear often? Are they present in your environment?

_____

_____

_____

_____

■ What shapes appear often? Are they present in your environment?

_____

_____

_____

_____

_____

■ What textures appear often? Are they present in your environment?

_____

_____

_____

_____

Now use the Wish List to note items you want to bring into your Flourishing Home. Use the Task Breakdown blueprint to manage the projects that come out of this blueprint.

_____

_____

_____

_____

_____

_____

_____

_____

_____

_____

_____

_____

_____

_____

_____

_____

_____

_____

_____

_____

_____

_____

_____

_____

## NATURE, VIEWS AND LIGHT BLUEPRINT

For all the critical living areas in your home, consider the impact of nature.

■ What views do you have to the outside from each vantage point?

_____

_____

_____

_____

_____

_____

■ Can the view be enhanced by adding a garden statue or trimming back a bush?

_____

_____

_____

_____

■ What is your exposure to natural light? Can that be adjusted to increase sunlight, reduce glare, or control temperature?

_____

_____

_____

_____

■ Can the same areas that allow natural light into your home be controlled to block out light and create optimal sleeping conditions?

_____

_____

_____

_____

■ Can the windows or doors be opened to the fresh air and the sounds of nature?

_____

_____

_____

_____

■ How do your views and vantage points change seasonally?

_____

_____

_____

_____

_____

_____

■ Do you want to bring natural elements into your home?

_____

_____

_____

■ What natural elements are already present?

_____

_____

_____

_____

Once you've answered these questions, review the section on biophilic responses for specific points that will springboard you into changes, adjustments and ideas of your own!

## COMMAND CENTRAL BLUEPRINT

Because the command central is critical to a Flourishing Home, it gets its own blueprint! Before you think about where to set it up, answer these questions.

What are the critical elements of your home that need to be organized? Consider work schedules, social events, sports practice and game schedules, school activities, home maintenance tasks, weekly chores, health and medical management.

- Do you need a grocery list to optimize healthy eating behaviors and nutrition?

- Do you volunteer for charities or nonprofit organizations? Do you conduct the work inside your home or on site with the charity?

- Do you have a system to help manage stress?

- Is the system you're currently using to pay bills, track schedules, or file important papers working?

- Are your tools easily accessible and centrally located?

- Is the command central system familiar to everyone in the home?

- Is the system simple and easy to use?

## TOWNHOUSE / CONDOMINIUM / APARTMENT BLUEPRINT

Frequently people think that the Flourishing Home concepts only apply to single-family homes. That's because so many designers, landscapers, furniture companies and appliance manufacturers focus on homeowners in their sales pitches. Nothing can be further from the truth! No matter where you live or how small your space, the exact same concepts apply. Apartments, condos and townhouses need hubs, hearts, refueling areas, transition zones, a sense of place, and attention to primes. In fact, small spaces can be the coziest of all Flourishing Homes!

Let's follow Sharon home to her apartment. At the end of her workday, she passes through the building's lobby, rides the elevator up, and walks down a hallway before reaching her front door. She might not be able to influence the public areas but they're preliminary transitions points. She can use triggering messages like *As I enter the lobby, I will take a deep breath to help me bring closure to the stressful work day. When I push the elevator button, I will remember to loosen my tense shoulders. When I walk through my apartment's door, I will know that I'm home and that I can relax.*

The moment she's inside the studio apartment, she can see the hub, heart and refueling areas. The room is the same soft blue as the evening sky during her favorite vacation. Pictures of laughing friends welcome her back. A narrow ledge and a few wall hooks hold her keys and her bag.

She moves a few feet to her home's heart and hub. A small refrigerator, microwave, cabinet and countertop gather in the kitchen heart. A compact set of measuring cups, spoons and a scale are at hand along with a set of appropriately sized serving dishes. When she opens her refrigerator, a large container of water and fresh fruit are the first things she sees. She places the mail on a countertop tray that serves as a portable hub for personal, financial and social organization.

A few feet further into the studio, she turns on her evening play list, lights a lavender candle, and sits by the window on a convertible couch bed accessorized with soft throws and pillows. Although she uses that spot to regroup after work, she recognizes the importance of sleep and splurged on the best possible bedding.

**Now it's your turn!**

- What are your preliminary transition points?

_____

_____

_____

_____

_____

- What are your entry transition points?

_____

_____

_____

_____

_____

- What are your routine transition points?

_____

_____

_____

_____

_____

- Where are your hubs?

_____

_____

_____

_____

_____

■ Where are your hearts?

_____

_____

_____

_____

_____

_____

■ Do you have the best possible tools on hand?

_____

_____

_____

_____

_____

■ How can you enhance your senses of place through primes, color, sounds and scent?

_____

_____

_____

_____

_____

■ Have you created the best possible refueling areas? _____

_____

_____

_____

_____

_____

## SEXY WORKING FORWARD, SEXY WORKING BACKWARDS BLUEPRINT

Sometimes in life we tackle things from the inside out or from the outside in. To put it another way, no one follows the same path as everyone else! Let's use that approach to discover what's sexy for you. If living your happiest and healthiest life leads you to a sexy, rock the world attitude, turn it around. Ask:

■ What's sexy to me?

_____

_____

_____

_____

■ How are my health and happiness helping me feel awesome?

_____

_____

_____

_____

■ How are my health and happiness blocking me from that awesome feeling?

_____

_____

_____

_____

After you've defined what sexiness is, flip the questions to explore each area of your wellness and wellbeing through the lens of sexiness:

■ How are my eating behaviors affecting my sexiness?

_____

_____

_____

_____

- How is my sexiness affecting my eating behaviors?

_____

_____

_____

- How is my nutrition affecting my sexiness?

_____

_____

_____

- How is my sexiness affecting my nutrition?

_____

_____

_____

- How does my personal time-out space affect my sexiness?

_____

_____

_____

- How does my sexiness affect my personal time-out space?

_____

_____

_____

- Add your own questions here:

_____

_____

_____

_____

_____

_____

## HOME ALTAR BLUEPRINT

■ What parts of your spiritual being are in need of support?

_____

_____

_____

_____

_____

■ If you were to write an affirmation that supports your spiritual wellness, what would it say?

_____

_____

_____

_____

_____

■ What kinds of things would symbolically represent the different parts of your affirmation?

_____

_____

_____

_____

_____

■ How can you bring them together in your home to create a unified statement?

_____

_____

_____

_____

_____

## Kitchen Inventory Blueprint

- Measuring Spoons: On hand? Easily accessible? _____
- Measuring Cups: On hand? Easily accessible? _____
- Kitchen Scale: On hand? Easily accessible? _____
- Clear storage containers? _____
- Solid storage containers? _____
- Single size storage containers? _____

**Place at eye level in the refrigerator:**
- Fresh fruits
- Fresh vegetables
- Precut fruit and veggie trays
- Low-calorie sauces and dressings

**Place at eye level in the pantry:**
- Whole grain rice
- Whole grain rice alternatives like quinoa or spelt
- Healthy snacks like turkey jerky, single servings of nuts, vacuum-dried fruit bits

**Reduce the number of snack options in the refrigerator and pantry**

**Plate size:**
- Variety of sizes to enhance portion control

**Plates**
- Variety of colors to enhance the food's visual impact

**Known capacities (consider marking the underside of each dish with a permanent marker):**
- Serving dish for 1 cup
- Serving dish for 1/2 cup
- Serving dish for 1/4 cup

**Beverage containers:**
- How many ounces does each type hold? _____
- Is water easily accessible? _____

**Cooking Tools:**

- Blender
- Steamer
- Oil spritzer
- Slow cooker

**Other:**

_____

_____

_____

_____

_____

_____

_____

_____



**Environment Influences**

- Lighting: Bulbs between 60 and 75 watts
- Sensory Balance: Eliminate visual overload by eliminating clutter and chaos

**Where do you eat?**

_____

_____

_____

_____

_____

**Plate meals before they come to the table (except vegetables)**

**Positive primes:**

_____

_____

_____

_____

_____

_____

_____

_____

_____

_____

_____

**Negative primes:**

_____

_____

_____

_____

_____

_____

_____

_____

_____

_____

_____

_____

# FUTURE OF THE FLOURISHING HOME

*T*hroughout this book, I've encouraged you to put yourself first, use blue sky thinking, adapt creative solutions, and mix and match the ideas and techniques I've developed while working one-on-one with clients. Now I'm going to give you an idea of exactly what can happen when you create a true Flourishing Home.

Jennifer wanted more time for activities that made her feel energized, healthy and fit. At the top of her list was more time to walk in her local parks and to enjoy cooking for her family of four. Among the other activities that would help her thrive emotionally were reading and the occasional yoga class with friends. Job demands, her family's schedule and managing her home were obstacles to feeling happy, healthy and, you guessed it, sexy. It was tough to perform at her best.

We began by laying a strong foundation. We explored her values and those of her family. She gained clarity about activities that were truly a priority to her, each member of her household, and the family as a whole. Through our discussions and by using the blueprints, she was able to reflect deeply on her needs, goals and desires. She identified the activities that would create a thriving environment and what an ideal blue-sky world would look like. The ultimate goal was laid out in a mission statement during our first session.

*As a family, we will strive to communicate about our daily lives. We will work at keeping a sense of humor and laughter, and will view life as a series of learning experiences and adventures. We will work at maintaining these priorities: Be grateful for simple joys and find excitement in new opportunities.*

She also clarified her own guiding principles. In order to thrive the best way possible, she wanted to make spiritual care a priority by walking in nature and reading inspirational books. Using the family and self mission statements, she lined up the goals we would achieve by having her home environment enhance her wellness and wellbeing.

1. Create an environment for comfortable family dinners (communication)
2. Make daily walk a priority (self care, exercise)
3. Enhance reading area to aide in refueling the spirit

I asked her to create an inspiration board. At our next session, we discussed the themes that had appeared, the colors that recurred, which of the aspects on the board were already present in her home, and which had not yet been added to her environment. She had an a-ha! moment when she realized that soft textures from downy pillows and fluffy white comforters took center stage. Soft hues with clean, modern lines were apparent, and the word *simple* appeared in two corners.

We discussed how her home functioned as a whole and how each room functioned. We explored what was working well in the rooms. She told me what her eyes were drawn to in each room and whether those elements evoked positive or negative feelings. We compared the characteristics on her board with those in her home. She quickly began to compile a wish list for things she wanted to bring into her home. Among the first was a new down comforter.

She also wrote down specific tasks that would help her accomplish her goals. She realized that the green color of her bedroom, where she liked to read, was different from the whites and off-whites on her inspiration board, so her to-do list began with repainting the bedroom. The chaos of the laundry room, she realized, left her feeling overwhelmed and burdened with upkeep. That feeling, in turn, kept her from taking that daily walk.

Another important step in Jennifer's journey was brainstorming possible strategies, tools and tactics so the family had a comfortable place for healthy meals. As a group, they came up with five to seven meals everyone enjoyed and that everyone could help prepare. The entrees were scheduled by coordinating everyone's activities and making dinners a priority.

Her kitchen inventory uncovered the need for a scale as well as small serving dishes for favorite family snacks, so she added those items to her wish-list. The family adopted the new strategies and pitched in right away with the back pocket meals. Having the tools on hand to support meal preparation decreased stress. In the end, it created more time to do the things that helped Jennifer thrive. She was able to find more time for those nature walks!

Over the next few weeks, she took a giant leap forward along with a few baby steps. She repainted her bedroom off-white, then added a fluffy comforter and two downy pillows. The bedroom, her personal space for spiritual refueling and sleep, was transformed into a cocoon of simplicity. She also got rid of a few negative primes and gathered positive primes on a side table that functioned as a miniature home altar. It included a family vacation picture, three of her favorite books, and a rosemary/peppermint candle.

Utilizing *The Flourishing Home's* definition of clutter, she tweaked her functional hub and laundry room in one short afternoon. She got rid of unused, torn, stained and outgrown clothing. After space had been freed up, the room functioned better and created less stress. This single act also freed up more time to read, walk and cook. By the end of our work together Jennifer was happier, healthier, and had that rock-the-world sexy attitude. She felt better, her family grew closer, and the daily chores became less of a burden for everyone… the promise of every Flourishing Home!

While that blue sky experience reflects only a little of what a truly Flourishing Home can accomplish, life will intervene. On your way to building and maintaining a happy, healthy, sexy life, you'll run into obstacles. Even I do! While writing the last chapter of this book, my mother fell and broke several bones. My husband, my best friend and a true partner in the game of life, began to run a fever…a rare occurrence in our decades together. My son was facing a major life decision that would have repercussions no matter what he chose. All this happened within a single thirty-six hour period!

Add work and family obligations like helping my eldest with a college search, physicals and dental checkups for the younger two, and the daily upkeep of a family of five, I found myself stressed. Even putting myself in time out and getting a good night's sleep didn't tip the scale to the positive side in many areas of my wellness and wellbeing. None of these issues is unusual or unexpected and they certainly aren't extreme. But the real world is full of obstacles and challenges. The moments when the stars align are fleeting and rare.

As I stated in the beginning, *The Flourishing Home* isn't a magic pill for weight loss, it's not the panacea that will eliminate stress, it can't solve your financial problems or fix a personal relationship. It can support your efforts to do all this and more. Creating your own Flourishing Home can support all the elements and combinations of wellness and wellbeing! Your home environment can help you achieve your heart's desires...and it should and can be set up to enhance your happiness, your health, and a rock the world outlook. By living the Flourishing Home lifestyle, you'll thrive with authenticity, vigor, vibrancy, and a sexy attitude.

If there's a way to make life easier, sign me up! Why make it hard if there's a tool, tactic, hint, solution, idea or answer that can help? That's what I hope you've found in this book. Maybe the tool or tactic was straightforward. Maybe a kitchen scale helped you realize just how much of your favorite foods you were eating. That in turn brought mindfulness and enjoyment to the physical act of nurturing your body, which in turn meant you shed a few pounds.

Then you felt just enough empowerment to walk a couple of nights a week. Those walks helped you maintain the weight loss and brought your cholesterol down, thereby decreasing your chance of metabolic disorders. Your friends joined you on the walks and the time spent together has enhanced your positive relationships with other human beings. They've also told you about a volunteer opportunity that engages your sense of purpose. Often one or two changes will have a positive domino effect.

Maybe a tactic suggested in the book can enhance your health and happiness. You employ a tactic to reduce stress that also leaves you with more time to do the things you love. Maybe getting a little more organized through tackling primary clutter frees you to finally take that art class. The class refuels you spiritually and makes you happier and more relaxed. The happiness and stress reduction filters down to those you love. One small tweak can domino into a happier you!

While I hope the book has provided a tool, tactic or idea spark, you are ultimately your own life expert. You don't have to walk the hard road to find the stars aligning in your universe of wellness and wellbeing. This book makes your life easier by getting your Flourishing Home to work for you. You owe it to yourself to become a little more mindful, gain clarity on your needs and goals, and be inspired to live your best life as a happy, healthy, sexy flourishing person!